The Fairy Races of the British Isles

By Robert Lee (Skip) Ellison
Illustrations by Rhiannon Ellison

Illustrated by Rhiannon Ellison
Cover Design: Willow Nimfeach
Published by Dragon's Keep Publishing
East Syracuse, NY

ISBN: 1497430232

ISBN-13: 978-1497430235

Table of Contents

DEDICATION

This book is dedicated to everyone who has a thirst for knowledge about the Faeries. We know that they are real, and we always want more information about them. In this book, I hope to present that information.

ACKNOWLEDGMENTS

I'd like to thank all of the people that have scanned in out-of-print books to make them available to the general population via the Internet. Without their work, and those books being available, this project would never have come to completion. I would also like to thank the many people who have gone out to interview people about their knowledge and interactions of the Faeries. It was this work which led to what we know today.

1 WHAT ARE THE FAERIES?

This book started out as a workshop in 2008. I had been doing a lot of reading in old out-of-print books on mythology and folklore from the British Isles, and I was amazed at the amount of information, much of it gleaned from firsthand accounts, of the many different kinds (races) of faeries there. One advantage of reading this type of books is that many of them are available for free online. As is often the case, this reading led me to more and more books; and after a bit, I found I had amassed a large collection of stories about the Fair Folk, a term they much prefer over Faeries, and that it was time to share what I had found.

Since much of this information comes from folklore studies and books, I'll start this chapter by talking a little first about folklore. W.Y. Evans-Wentz, writing in one of the best books on the subject of the faeries in the British Isles gives a good description on how folklore, as well as other subjects, are used in his study:

> "In this study, which is first of all a folk-lore study, we pursue principally an anthropo-psychological method of interpreting the Celtic belief in faeries, though we do not hesitate now and then to call in the aid of philology; and we make good use of the evidence offered by mythologies, religions, metaphysics, and physical sciences. Folk-lore, a century ago was considered beneath the serious consideration of scholars; but there has come about a complete reversal of scholarly opinion, for now it is seen that the beliefs of the people, their legends, and their songs are the source of nearly all literatures, and that their institutions and customs are the origin of those of modern times. And,

> to-day, to the new science of folk-lore--which, as Mr. Andrew Lang says, must be taken to include psychical research or psychical sciences, archaeology, anthropology, and comparative mythology and religion are indispensable. Thus folklore offers the scientific means of studying man in the sense meant by the poet who declared that 'the proper study of mankind is man.'"[1]

This was written in 1911, and the study of folklore has progressed greatly since then. There is now a classification system for "fairy tales" and other types of oral history stories. It is called the Aarne–Thompson tale type index, and Wikipedia says this about the system:

> "The Aarne-Thompson tale type index is a multivolume listing designed to help folklorists identify recurring plot patterns in the narrative structures of traditional folktales, so that folklorists can organize, classify, and analyze the folktales they research. First developed by Antti Aarne (1867-1925) and published as *Verzeichnis der Märchentypen* in 1910, the tale type index was later translated, revised, and enlarged by Stith Thompson (1885-1976) in 1928 and again in 1961."[2]

The stories we are mainly interested in here are classified in the 300-749 category range. They deal with the supernatural - the creatures, encounters, relatives, tasks, etc. The use of a coherent classification system has allowed scholars to pursue this field of study extensively over the years since Evan-Wentz wrote the above, and there are many journal articles that have been produced which provide us very useful information about the faeries. While the journal articles are helpful, I feel that it is reading the tales for

[1] WY Evans-Wentz, *The Fairy-Faith in Celtic Countries*, XIV.
[2] "Aarne–Thompson Classification System - Wikipedia, the Free Encyclopedia."

yourself that helps the most. While they many times do not come out and describe the type of fairy, you can piece together descriptions from the similar tales.

I'll continue this chapter with a question - What are the faeries? Overall, this is a very good question, and one that has many answers! Some people believe that they are members of ancient races, which at one point in our history occupied the Earth with the human races. Others believe that they are beings that exist in a parallel universe, which touches upon ours at certain times. Still others feel they are the remnants of alien races that crashed to Earth in a long past time. While the actual answer is unknown, we do have a lot of evidence to show that they are around us. Looking back in the folklore records, we see many examples of people who have seen, and visited with the faeries. I'll be discussing these ideas on what the faeries actually are in more detail in chapter 10 - conclusions.

Let us continue this discussion by looking at what others have said the faeries are. In an article in the journal "Folklore," R.U. Sayee quotes another early author, E.S. Hartland who was writing in "The Science of Fairy Tales," as saying:

> "The chief distinction of the faeries from men, according to Hartland, is their unbounded magical powers. This statement probably contains a good deal of the truth. Faeries have the power of appearing and disappearing, apparently at will; and they are usually regarded as some kind of spirit, though, like spirits in other parts of the world, they are not thought of as being purely unsubstantial. They pinch lazy maids black and blue and jostle people who get in their way, just as in the islands of Polotu and Tonga there are mischievous sprites who trip up the natives and pinch them in the dark."[3]

---

[3] R. U. Sayce, "The Origins and Development of the Belief in Fairies," 99.

Mr. Sayee continues by saying:

> "There is nothing so far that will help us to distinguish faeries from other spirits; nor will their size give us much help. They are frequently described as being very small, but there are many stories in which they are regarded as of ordinary size; people often mistake them for normal beings, and marriages between mortals and faeries are not at all uncommon. Nor can their shape be used as a criterion of their fairyhood, since they have the power of changing it and can appear as birds or mammals."[4]

From these two quotes, two things stand out. First the faeries are very magical creatures, and second, their size may vary wildly. We see in many of the old books that the descriptions and names vary wildly as well, which has led me to the proposition that there are many different races, or types, or species of faeries in the British Isles. So let's look at what names were used for the faeries, to see if that will help answer the question of what they are?

Names for the Faeries

One of the longest list of names for the faeries that I have found in one book can be found in "The Handbook of Folklore," written in 1890 by George Laurence Gomme. He tells us:

> "The belief in spirits which assume a form and possess characteristics more or less like mankind is prevalent nearly everywhere. These spirits appear either as very diminutive or as gigantic; as nimble, merry, and clever; or as heavy, plodding, and stupid. The name generally given to them is that of fairy or goblin.

[4] Ibid., 100.

Special names have been given to these spirits, and the following list is perhaps tolerably perfect. Wherever one of these names is applied to faeries or goblins it should be noted, and where other names exist they should be recorded. The names are - Adamastor, Alastor, Amadeus, Auld Ane, Auld Clootie, Auld Hornie, Banshee, Barguest or Bhargeist, Befann, Blackman, Blinkin, Belleus, Bertha Frau or Frau Frecht, Black John, Bloody Bones, Bloody Cap, Blue, Boggart, Bogie, Bogle, Brown Dwarf, Brownie, Brownie Catch, Capelthwaite, Chappie, Cloutie, Cob, Cluri-Caune, Dobie, Duergar, Dunters, Dunnie, Eckhardt, Elberich, Erl King or Konig, Flibberty Gibbet, Flying Dutchman, Frater-eto, Freischutz, Friar Rush, Fost Jack, Gabble Retchets, Gabriel Hounds, Gargantea, Gingerbread Giles, Gloriana, Goldeman, Goodman or Gudeman, Good Neighbour, Good People, Grand Gousier or Gangausier, Grim, Grizell Gridigut, Habetrot, Hardname, Hedley Kow, Hellequin, Hendrie Craig, Herlething, Hob, Hobany, Hobbidi-Dance, Hobberdi-Dance, Hobgoblin, Hodeken, Hop-o'-my-Thumb, Horner Jack, Hudkin, Hiegon, Jack with the Lantern, Jenny Greenteeth, Kill-moulis, Knockers, Knop, Knap, Kobold, Lamkin, Lammikin, Levana, Licke, Linkin, Lilith or Leles, Lull, MacKeeler, Man in the Moon, Man of Peace, Morgutte, Master Leonard, Melissa, Morgunte, Mumbo Jumbo, News, Nick, Nickle Ben, Nippen, Number Nip, Oberon, Obedient, Old Bendy, Old Bogy, Old Gentleman, Old Harry, Old Man of the Sea, Old Nick, Old Scratch, On Risk, Oschaert, Padfoot, Peek in the Crown, Peg o'Nell, Peg Powler, Peg a Lantern,

> Phooka, Phynnoderee, Pig Wiggin, Pixie, Powriet, Puck, Pyenocket, Quilp, Redcap, Redman, Robert the Jakis, Robert the Rule, Robert des Bois, Robin Goodfellow, Rosie, Rubeza, Rupert Knight, Sack and Sugar, Saunders the Red Reaver, Scantlie Mab, Shefro, Sib, Silky, Skow, Smack, Smalkin or Smulkin, Spunkie, Swain the old Duergar, The Roaring Lion, Thief of Hell, Thomas the Feary, Thrumpin Tib, Toticellus, Tocabatto, Troll, Vinegar Tom, Voland Squire, Wag-at-the-Wa', Wait upon Herself, Wap, Wild Huntsman, Will with the Wisp, Winn, Wryneck, Yeth Hounds."[5]

While I am not going to cover all of these names in this book, I will be talking about a few of them. As you can see here, the faeries have been called by many names. In France, the modern word *"fée"* likely came from the Old French word *"féer."* This meant "to enchant" and is probably from the Latin word *"fatare."* This enchantment refers to the aeries ability to "cloud" the vision of humans and make them see whatever the faeries wanted.

The French terms led to the English word "faerie," which encompasses both the realm of faerie and to be enchanted by the faeries, as in "you've been brushed by faeries." The English terms "fey" and "fairy" usually refer only to individual faeries.[6] According to the Merriam Webster Collegiate Dictionary, both faerie and fairy are pronounced the same - \'fer-ē\.[7]

Another term used in English to mean fairy is "elf", especially in older usage. To some people, the elves were a different race from the faeries, but this is a modern day interpretation, mainly after J.R. Tolkien's usage in the "Lord of the Rings." Originally, the word came from the Anglo-Saxons *"alfar."*

---

[5] Gomme, George Laurence, *The Handbook of Folklore*, 30–32.

[6] Ellen Phillips, *The Enchanted World: Fairies and Elves*, 10.

[7] Merriam-Webster Dictionary, "Fairy - Free Merriam-Webster Dictionary"; Merriam-Webster Dictionary, "Faerie - Free Merriam-Webster Dictionary."

To the Norse people, the ancestors of the Anglo-Saxons, the *alfar* were divided into two groups, the *liosálfar* and the *döckálfar*. The *liosálfar* were the light, or good elves, and dwelt in the regions of the air and are the ones who helped the humans. We hear in *Saemund's Edda*, the Elder or Poetic Edda, that the home of the light elves is in *Alf-heim*. The *Aesir* gave *Alf-heim* to Frey on his birth. "*Alf-heim* the gods to Frey, gave in days of yore, for a tooth gift." He ruled there benevolently and the elves gladly did his bidding, for they were pre-eminently a beneficent race.[8]

The *döckálfar* were the dark, or bad elves and dwelt in the regions of the Earth. These dark elves were also known as dwarfs in English, with their kingdoms underground. They are the faeries who stood against the humans. It is said that the dark elves were formed from the maggots emerging from the corpse of the giant Ymir.[9]

It is usually considered bad luck to refer directly to the faeries, so each culture has developed their own euphemisms for the tribes of faeries that live in their lands. This usually helps prevent the mischief that they have been noted for.

For example, in Ireland they are referred to as "The Good Folk," "The People of Peace," "Wee Folk," "The Mother's Blessing," "The Gentry," or the like.

In Scotland, they are referred to as "The Still Folk" or "The Silent Moving Folk."

In Brittany, they are called "The *Corrigan*," "Phantoms of the Dead," "*nos Bonnes Mères les Fées* (Our Good Mothers The Faeries)," "The *Fées*," "*Fetes* (Fates)," or "*Fions* (Sprites)."

On the Isle of Man, you may hear "*Mooinjer-Veggey* or *Sleih Beggey* (The Little People,)" "*Cloan ny Moyrn* (Children of Pride)," "Themselves," "Little Boys," or "Little Fellas," and "*Guillyn Veggey* (The Little Boys.)"

And in Wales they are called "The Fair Folk," "The Fair Family," "*Dynon Buch Teg* (The Fair Small People)," "*Plant Rhys Ddwfn*

8 Guerber, *Myths of the Norsemen*, 117.

9 Ellen Phillips, *The Enchanted World: Fairies and Elves*, 10–11.

(Children of Rhys Ddwfn," *"Verry Volk,"* or *"Bendith y Mamau,"* (The Mothers' Blessing). Another term used in Wales is *"Ellyll,"* but since this just means elf or goblin, or demon, I really don't think it's a euphemism. I'll cover this term, as used for a specific type of faerie, more in chapter 7 on Wales.

Overall, the names are not much help right now for our original question, but as we work through the different types of faeries, we will learn more to help us find our answer. Next I'd like to talk a little about the broad classifications of the faerie types.

Classes of Faeries

First there are the trooping faeries. They are the faeries that band together and move around the landscape as a 'tribe" or "clan." There are many tales that deal with the battles between troops of faeries from neighboring counties, or of people building a house on a "faerie road" and the problems they have. I'll be talking about some specific examples in the chapters on the different countries. In Scotland, the trooping faeries are divided up into two categories, the "good faeries" and the "bad faeries" if you will. The faeries belonging to the *seelie* court, or blessed court, are the "good faeries," the faeries willing to help humanity. They are the equivalent to the "light elves" in the Scandinavian countries. On the other hand, we have the *unseelie* court, or the "bad faeries." They are the equivalent to the "dark elves" in the Scandinavian countries.

In Ireland, the name *Daoine Sídhe* is the name given to the people of the *Tuatha Dé Danann* after they went underground into the faerie mounds. They are also known as the "Dwellers of the Faerie Mounds," or the *Sídhe Mór* (Great *Sídhe*).

One of the *Daoine Sídhe* and its current king, is Finnbheara. He is said to rule all the faerie realms in Ireland from his home, or "rath" in Knockmagha, west of Tuam in Co. Galway. He is known for his love of games of skill, and his love of women. Even though his wife, Úna, is the most beautiful woman in both the mortal and faerie realms, he still finds time for other lovers, with his wife's consent. In addition, of course, Úna does the same.[10] The Irish also divide the trooping faeries into "land faeries," called *Sheoques*, which means little faeries in Irish, and "water faeries," called *Merrows*, which means sea-maid in Irish.[11] The Welsh equivalent of the *Daoine Sidhe* is the *Tylwyth Teg*, and that name means "The Beautiful People" or the "Faerie People."

We also have the solitary faeries, which usually stay by themselves and away from people. Many of the "races" of faeries I'll be talking about belong to this class of faeries. Their main pleasure in life is to find ways to create mischief and harm to people, the "bad faeries" in other words. Some people think that these faeries are actually the vengeful ghosts or spirits of mortals, but I, and many others, think that is wrong.

They are not likely to be found in groups with other faeries as the trooping faeries are. Although they have some of the same powers as the trooping faeries, such as the ability to turn invisible, or the ability to change shape, they have tended to stay well away from humans, unless they can catch them alone!

It has been said that they are the "peasants" of the faerie races, while the trooping faeries were the "aristocrats." In Irish, both the solitary faeries and some of the lessor trooping faeries are known by the collective name of the *Sídhe Beag* (Little *Sídhe*).

While the evidence for faeries covers many lands around the World, in this book I will be concentrating on the British Isles & Brittany. By that I mean, in alphabetical order, Brittany, England, Ireland, the Isle of Man, Scotland, and Wales. I fully understand that there are many ways to divide the countries up, but this is simply the one that I choose to simplify the work.

---

10 Larkin, *Faeries*, 42–46; MacKillop, *Dictionary of Celtic Mythology*, 374.
11 WB Yeats, *Irish Fairy Tales - Yeats 1892*, 223.

Scottish Ghillie Dhu

2 BRITTANY[12]

12 "Brittany Map."

Ankou

Our first fairy from Brittany is found all over the area and is called the *ankou*. The *ankou* is also called the "Death in Skeleton" or "King of the Dead." There are a couple different references to the *ankou*.

In the book, "Legends and Romances of Brittany" by Lewis Spence, he tells us that the *ankou*, in the form of a skeleton, travels around the countryside in a cart collecting the souls of the newly dead; almost like the character of "Death," in the Terry Pratchett Discworld series. It is said that the peasants of the area fear the sound of an axle creaking in the night, fearing it may be the *ankou* after someone in their house.[13]

Another story, which I've only found in a footnote in the book "The Fairy-Faith in Celtic Countries" by W.Y. Evans-Wentz[14], talks about how each parish has its own *ankou*, who is the last man to die in the parish during the year. He then serves as the *ankou* until the start of the next year when he is replaced.

There is also a discrepancy in the sex of this faerie. In the first story, it is said that the *ankou* is female and is likely the remnant of a pre-Christian Goddess of the dead. In the last story, the *ankou* is presented as male, hence the term "King of the Dead." In some churches in the area, statuettes of the *ankou* can be found, and they are usually stylized skeletons.

---

[13] Lewis Spence, *Legends and Romances of Brittany*, 102–103.
[14] "P. 218 Footnote - Ankou."

Crions, Courils, and Gorics

Our next faeries are types of gnomes or dwarfs that are associated with standing stones and stone circles. They are also said to inhabit the remains of Druid monuments and ancient castles. It is said that they are about one to two feet in height and very strong. Legends say that is was their strength that raised the stone monuments.

Of the three names they are known by: *crions*, *courils*, or *gorics*, the latter is the more prevalent one. The *courils* are peculiar to the ruins of Tresmalouen, while the *crions* are found throughout the area. All of these faeries are fond of dancing in the stone circles and the fairy rings found throughout the area.

Lewis Spence, again writing in the book "Legends and Romances of Brittany" tells us that "Carnac is sometimes alluded to in Breton as '*Ty C'harriquet*,' 'the House of the *Gorics*.'"[15] He tells us that each night, the *gorics* dance around the mound and if any human should come upon them, they are forced to join the dance until they pass out from exhaustion.

Like many other similar types, these faeries are also known as "treasure keepers," the faeries who guard large hoards of treasures.

It has been said that on rare occasions, a human who has done them a favor, will be allowed to take some of their gold, but no more than a handful. If they try to take more than that, both the faerie and the gold will disappear and never be seen again!

[15] Lewis Spence, *Legends and Romances of Brittany*, 98–100.

Korrigan

Our next type of faerie is both a specific type, and a generic name for many of the faeries of Brittany. Their name is spelled either *korrigan* or *corrigan.* As a specific type, the *korrigan* is said to be a water faerie that inhabits fountains or wells and is almost always female. She will appear to people who come to her fountain and ask for her aid, but if the supplicant is a young male, then the price she takes may very well be the love of the man forever!

She is said to have been found most often in the forests and towns of the mythological "Forest of Broceliande." This name was given in the early stories as a place where the faeries dwelt, and the Arthurian characters remained hidden from sight. It is also given as the site of Merlin's tomb. It is said that the *korrigan* has the ability to change the appearance of anything around her. Usually appearing only at night, she has often been seen surrounded by a "court" of nine nymphs, all of exceedingly great beauty, in luxurious surroundings, with a banquet of fine and rare foods to offer to any human who came upon her.

Evan-Wentz tells us that the name is applied as a term for most of the faeries, but he is alone in this assertion. He tells us that:

> "It is the *corrigan* race, however, which, more than *fées* or faeries, forms a large part of the invisible inhabitants of Brittany; and this race of *corrigans* and *nains* (dwarfs) may be made to include many kinds of *lutins*, or as they are often called by the peasant, *follets* or *esprits follets* (playful elves)."[16]

[16] WY Evans-Wentz, *The Fairy-Faith in Celtic Countries*, 206; MacKillop, *Dictionary of Celtic Mythology*, 256.

Mari Morgan

The Morgan is said to be the queen of the sea-folk who live in the channel between Brittany and England. While not many stories are told about the sea-folk themselves, there are several about their queen. It is said that Morgan, or Mari Morgan as she is known in Breton, was the daughter of the King of *Ys*. She is named Dahut in most of the modern tales.

Ys was a legendary city that had been built on an island, below sea level, in the sea off the Brittany coast. It was protected from flooding by a series of dikes. One night, during a raging storm and at the height of the full moon, Dahut stole the key to the main dike from her father and opened it, allowing the city to sink beneath the waves. The inhabitants of *Ys* became the sea-folk, and Morgan became their queen after her father died in the flooding.[17]

Legend tells us that the city did not lose any of its splendor under the sea, but grew more beautiful as its people adapted to life under the water. It is told that Morgan climbs to the rocks above the water line each evening, and you can hear her bemoaning her fate and looking for forgiveness for her great mistake.

Other tales tell us that while many mortal men are attracted to her because of her singing, it is her fate that whenever she touches a mortal man, that man will die instantly.

[17] MacKillop, *Dictionary of Celtic Mythology*, 381–382.

Mourioche

Our next faerie type has been seen all over the area of Brittany and is most often seen in the shape of a young horse, although it has been said that they can take the shape of any animal. They appear to be much like the *phooka* of Ireland, and the *kelpie* of Scotland, in that they will harm humans if they get the chance.

In "Legends and Romances of Brittany," Lewis Spence tells us:

> "He is especially dangerous to children, and Breton babies are often chided when noisy or mischievous with the words: 'e good, now, the *Mourioche* is coming!' Of one who appears to have received a shock, also, it is said: 'He has seen the *Mourioche*.'"[18]

Another tale tells us that the *mourioche* is a werewolf like fairy that dwells in a pond near the castle of *Beauchene* in *Langrolay*, France. *Langrolay-sur-Rance*, as its known today, is located in the *Côtes-d'Armor* section of Brittany in the Northwest of France. The *mourioche* was said to have terrorized the people of the area until it was killed by Jehan, a young lord of the castle.[19]

[18] Lewis Spence, *Legends and Romances of Brittany*, 101.
[19] "Mourioche."

Nain

The *nains* are said to be the most fearsome of the faeries in Brittany. They are said to have been the models for the gargoyles that are found on the medieval cathedrals, with cat-like claws on their front feet, and satyr-like hooves on their back feet. They like to watch as humanity passes below them, always looking for a careless human that can be taken unawares.

At night, it is said they can be found dancing around the lonely dolmens. If any human finds them, he will be forced to join them in their dance and will be dead before the year is out. One of their favorite activities during the day, is to trap foolish humans into an exchange of services which results in their receiving "fairy gold." Lewis Spence tells us:

> "The housewife receives gold from a fairy for services rendered, and carefully places it in a drawer. A day when she requires it arrives, but, alas! when she opens the cabinet to take it out she finds nothing but a small heap of withered leaves. It is such money that the *nains* manufacture in their subterranean mints--coin which bears the fairy impress of glamourie for a space, but on later examination proves to be merely dross."[20]

[20] Lewis Spence, *Legends and Romances of Brittany*, 98; See MacKillop, *Dictionary of Celtic Mythology*, 302 for more information.

Sand Yan y Tad

Our next faerie, the *sand yan y tad,* which means Saint John and Father in Bretton, is the Brittany version of the English will-o-the-wisp, the Irish water *sheerie,* and the Welsh *ellylldan.* This faerie is described in the tales as appearing as a person with small fires at the ends of their fingers. It was said that the fires appeared to be spinning, and this caused the people to try and get near to better see what they were.

Other tales describe them as hideous beings of human height, with a large gaping mouth and a body that is covered in long hair. They also have spinning wheels of fire at their fingertips, and move about by leaping repeatedly like grasshoppers. Like all of the will-o-the-wisp types of faeries, their main goal was to lure people into the bogs and swamps, and then drown them or leave them to slowly find their way out.[21]

[21] Wirt Sikes, *British Goblins: Welsh Folk-Lore, Fairy Mythology, Legends and Traditions,* 18–19.

Teurst

It is in the district of *Morlaix*, in the *Finistère* section of Brittany in Northwest France, where we find our next type of faerie, the *teurst*. They are another fearsome type, said to be large, black, ugly "creatures" who haunt lonely moors and glens. In some of the tales, they are the personification of the Devil, and in others, their main characteristic is that they prevent the Devil from attacking humans.

Some of the tales suggest that the *teurst* could change its shape into many different forms of animals, to lull humans into coming closer to it. In "Legends and Romances of Brittany," Lewis Spence tells us that in other areas of Brittany, it was also known as *teursta poulict*, and *Teus* or *Bugelnoz*. In this latter form, it was said to wear white and be active in the early morning hours between midnight and two AM.[22]

[22] Lewis Spence, *Legends and Romances of Brittany*, 100.

Youdic

As well as being the name for our next type of faeries, *youdic* is also the name of one part of a peat bog in the *Montagnes d'Arrée* mountain range in Western Brittany. This peat bog, which is called the *Yeun*, has always been a source of fear among the inhabitants of the area, and for a long time, was thought to be one of the gateways to Hell itself. Part of its mystique is that while it looks like several large fields covered in heather, parts of those fields overlay treacherous, quicksand like sections of bog.

The people of the area used this section of the bog to dispose of animals they thought were "possessed by the Devil." Normally, one of the local priests and as many people as he needed to help him, would take the poor animals out and throw them into the quicksand below. Naturally, this resulted in many tales of the *youdic*, an animal that had escaped the clutches of the Devil, which roamed the area.

These faeries were described as "wild looking" large animals, that ran from the sight of man. I wouldn't blame them a bit for running away from people after having been thrown in quicksand and escaping![23]

[23] Ibid., 102–105.

3 ENGLAND[24]

[24] "Map-of-England-7."

Asrai

The first type of English faerie to talk about is the asrai. In the folktales, they are described as water faeries, similar to mermaids, only living in the large lakes instead of the sea. There are several differing descriptions of them. Some say they are as tall as humans, while others say they are short, only about two to four feet high. Most references to them say they are very beautiful, and either have pale white skin, or are translucent. Most observers have also said that they have webbed feet and hands, as well as green hair. An interesting observation is that they were only seen at night, and it is said that the touch of sunlight would cause them to turn into a pool of water and die. Legend also tells us that once every one hundred years, they would come to the surface to "look upon the moon." That is why in the counties of Cheshire and Shropshire, middle left of the map above, full moon nights are called "asrai nights."

It is said that they live for hundreds of years, while maintaining the youthful appearance of children. While the asrai didn't mind being seen by humans, they were deathly afraid of being captured by people. They knew that if they were captured, the sunlight would catch them and they would die. There is a tale told in Cheshire, about a fisherman who caught an asrai in his net. As he was trying to get her into his boat, she grabbed hold of his arm and begged for her life. He told people after, that her touch was so cold that his arm never got warm again.[25]

[25] The information about the tale is from: Simon Butler, "The Asrai."

Black Annis

Our next fairy is from near Leicester, located in the East Midlands of England in County Lancashire, and is called Black Annis. It is said that she would frequent the area around the Dane Hills, and had a cave near the top of the hill. While the asrai were harmless to humans, Black Annis is the first of the faerie types in England we will discuss who were anything but nice! According to legends, Black Annis would come down from the hills at night to steal children. If she caught one out alone at night, she would take them home, skin them alive and eat them, and then put their skin on the walls of her cave.[26] It was said that she had dug the cave out from solid rock with her bare hands, and it was called Black Annis's Bower by the locals.

She was described as being an old woman with only one eye, long claws, and a bluish face. One of her favorite places to stay and watch for humans in her area was the tops of large oaks trees. Speculation by the locals was that she was an ancient goddess who had ruled over the forests, but became angry with humans for cutting it down, and so took her revenge on any human she chanced upon.

She may also have been a shape-shifter. Some of the legends talk about her taking the shape of a great cat, which would stalk travelers in the area. This legend persisted until the middle of the 18th century.[27]

26 Time-Life Books, *The Enchanted World: Night Creatures*, 21.
27 Daniel Parkinson, "Black Annis | Mysterious Britain & Ireland."

Black Shuck

The Black Shuck, also called Old Shuck, Old Shock or simply Shuck, is one of the faerie dogs. It is found in the Norfolk, Suffolk, and East Anglia areas, found in the middle right of the map above. Like many of the faerie dogs, it is said that if you see him, you will die before the year is out.

His description is similar to other faerie dogs, large — the size of a calf or small horse, black in color, and with blazing red eyes. In some of the tales, it is said that he only has one red eye, set right in the center of his forehead. His howl is described as blood-curdling; and it is told that if you hear it, you should shut your eyes so you do not see it, for then you will die.

One of the early tales, from 1127 in one of the Anglo-Saxon Chronicles, talks about how these dogs travel with the Wild Hunt, as it travels the countryside looking for souls to take with it into the Otherworld.[28]

[28] "Black Shuck"; William Alfred Dutt, *Highways and Byways in East Anglia*, 216.

Boggart

Coming from the same area as Black Annis, our next type of faerie, the boggart, is well known to many people from the Harry Potter films. In England, this faerie was commonly found in the northeast counties of Yorkshire and Lancashire. Lancashire today reminds us of the prevalence of these faeries, with towns named Boggart's Clough and Boggart's Hole. This type of faerie is also found in all of the countries we will be discussing here except Brittany, with local names and stories for all of them, most of them particular to the country.

As portrayed in Harry Potter, the boggarts are small faeries that are known for their mischievous behavior. They would move things around, break dishes and other fragile things and be blamed for "the noises in the night!" Much of this type of activity is today described as being done by "poltergeist." It is said that they are invisible to human eyes, but that dogs and other animals can see them, and will watch them move about. Like the brownies I'll be talking about later, many times they were associated with specific families and houses. If the people who lived there left out offerings for them, they would be "good" and not cause too much trouble. If they were insulted though, they would leave the people, and cause many problems as they left.[29]

An interesting story about a boggart can be found in the book, "Traditions Superstitions and Folklore of Lancaster and the North of England," written by Charles Hardwick in 1872. As he tells it:

> "Referring to the famous boggart of Syke Luinb farm, near Blackburn, Mr. Wilkinson says:—
> 'When in a good humour, this noted goblin will milk the cows, pull the hay, fodder the cattle, harness the horses, load the carts, and stack the crops. When irritated by the utterance of some unguarded expression or marked

[29] Daniel Parkinson, "Boggart | Mysterious Britain & Ireland"; Thomas Crofton Croker, *Fairy Legends and Traditions of the South of Ireland*, 109–110.

> disrespect, either from the farmer or his servants, the cream mugs are then smashed to atoms; no butter can be obtained by churning; the horses and other cattle are turned loose, or driven into the woods; two cows will sometimes be found fastened in the same stall; no hay can be pulled from the mow; and all the while the wicked imp sits grinning with delight upon one of the cross beams in the barn. At other times the horses are unable to draw the empty carts across the farm yard; if loaded they are upset; whilst the cattle tremble with fear, without any visible cause. Nor do the inmates of the house experience any better or gentler usage. During the night the clothes are said to be violently torn from off the beds of the offending parties, whilst, by invisible hands, they themselves are dragged down the stone stairs by the legs, one step at a time, after a more uncomfortable manner than we need describe.'"[30]

He then goes on to tell us that the voice of the boggart is not that unpleasant. This section is talking about a boggart that lived with a farmer named George Cheetham on a farm near Manchester, in the town of Blackley. It was located in a deep valley called "Boggart Ho' Clough." He says:

> "This same boggart, however, had some jolly genial qualities. His voice, when he joined the household laughter, on merry tales being told and practical jokes indulged in, around the hearth at Christmastide, is described as 'small and shrill,' and as easily 'heard above the rest, like a baby's penny trumpet.'"[31]

---

[30] Charles Hardwick, *Traditions Superstitions and Folklore of Lancaster and the North of England*, 126–127.

[31] Ibid., 128.

We find another interesting story about a boggart, dealing with where he lives in the house, in the book "The Fairy Mythology " by Thomas Keightley, written in 1828. He tells us,

> "He [the boggart] here caused a good deal of annoyance, especially by tormenting the children in various ways. Sometimes their bread and butter would be snatched away, or their porringers of bread and milk be capsized by an invisible hand; for the Boggart never let himself be seen; at other times, the curtains of their beds would be. shaken backwards and forwards, or a heavy weight would press on and nearly suffocate them.
>
> The parents had often, on hearing their cries, to fly to their aid. There was a kind of closet, formed by a wooden partition on the kitchen-stairs, and a large knot having been driven out of one of the deal-boards of which it was made, there remained a hole. Into this one day the farmer's youngest boy stuck the shoe-horn with which he was amusing himself, when immediately it was thrown out again, and struck the boy on the head. The agent was of course the Boggart, and it soon became their sport (which they called "laking with Boggart")to put the shoe-horn into the hole and have it shot back at them."[32]

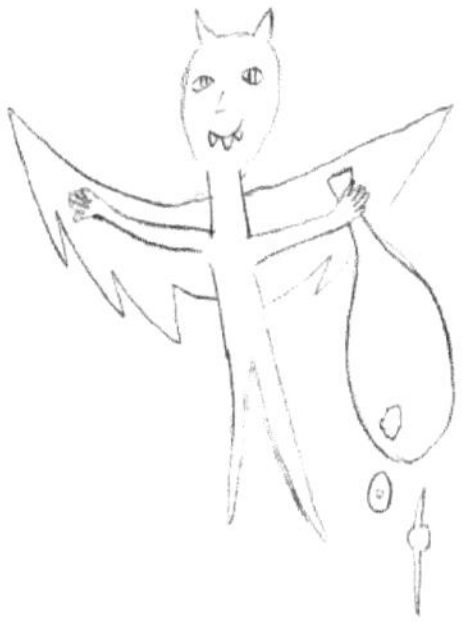

We will be talking more about the boggart in the rest of the countries we visit, but for now, let's move on to our next faerie.

[32] Keightley, Thomas, *The Fairy Mythology*, 307.

Boggle

The boggle is another mischievous faerie, and usually not trying "too much" to cause harm. One boggle of note, is called the Hedley Kow, and it was said that he lived in the village of Hedley, near Ebchester. Ebchester is located in County Durham, which is in the Northeast section of England, near the top right of the map at the start of this chapter.

In the stories told to us about the Hedley Kow, we hear that he liked to torment people. For example, if he found an old woman gathering sticks, he would take the form of a bundle of straw, which she would pick up and add to her bundle. After a bit, he would make himself gradually heavier and heavier, so the old woman wouldn't be able to carry it any further. Then the bundle of straw would "blow away in the wind" and make the old woman chase it while hearing the sound of laughter coming from it.

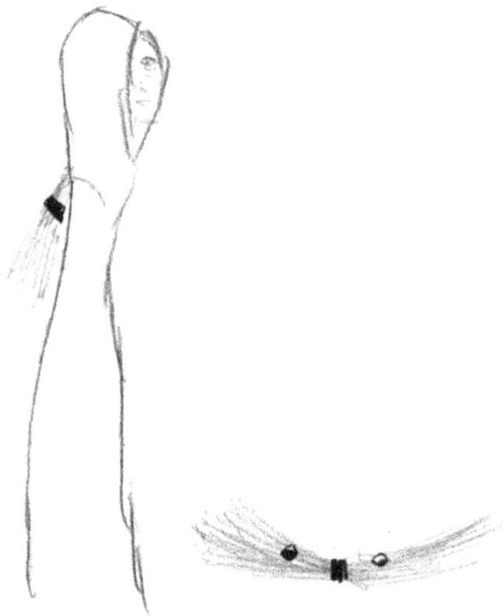

In the folk tale, "The Golden Ball," as told by Joseph Jacobs in "More English Fairy Tales," we hear that a group of boggles lived with, and served, a giant. After the hero of the story, a young boy, killed the giant, he stayed in the giant's house and found that the boggles had a golden ball that they played with. Eventually, he stole it from them and went back to his home and lived "happily ever after" as they say in the tales.[33]

We'll be hearing more about boggles in the section on Scotland.

[33] Joseph Jacobs, *More English Fairy Tales*, 12–15.

Brownie

Another well-known faerie from the Harry Potter series that was taken from the folktales of the countryside is the brownie. We see it in those movies as Dobby, the house elf. I feel that he is very well depicted based on the folklore of the brownies, including the scene where he is no longer bound to the house after he receives clothing from his master.

The brownies are usually seen as small, wrinkled brown beings, which are naked or wearing shaggy brown clothes. Some of the tales describe them as having large heads, big ears, and spindly bodies; but others describe them as more human like. They are very helpful beings that will do many small chores around the house as long as the family doesn't displease them. They are displeased if they are offered food or clothes **AS PAYMENT** for the work they do. It is fine if you leave food or whiskey out for them, you just have to be very careful not to give it **in thanks** for the work they do. You also need to be careful not to insult them or take their work for granted.

A good example of this is recorded in the book, "The Fairy Mythology." It is talking about a tale from the North of England where a brownie had come upon a house and liked the woman living there. He worked for her until she gave him clothes and then he left. It reads:

> "Coming to a farmer's house, he takes a liking to a 'good handsome maid,' that was there, and in the night does her work for her, at breaking hemp and flax, bolting meal, etc. Having watched one night and seen him at work, and observed that he was rather bare of clothes, she provided him with a waistcoat against the next night. But when he saw it he started and said:-
>
> Because thou layest me himpen bampen
> I will neither bolt nor stampen:
> 'Tis not your garments, new or old,
> That Robin loves: I feel no cold.

Had you left me milk or cream,
You should have had a pleasing dream:
Because you left no drop or crum,
Robin never more will come."[34]

Another example is from Hilton Hall where the brownie was called, "The Cauld Lad." This story tells us:

"The servants, however, resorted to the usual mode or banishing a Brownie: they left a green cloak and hood for him by the kitchen fire, and remained on the watch.
They saw him come in, gaze at the new clothes, try them on, and, apparently in great delight, go jumping and frisking about the kitchen. But at the first crow of the cock he vanished, saying -

'Here's a cloak, and here's a hood!
The Cauld Lad of Hilton will do no more good.'

And he never again returned to the kitchen; yet it was said that he might still be heard at midnight singing those lines in a tone of melancholy."[35]

It is said that they like to be in the houses of industrious people, and do not like laziness. This is illustrated by another story from "The Fairy Mythology," talking about the women brownies. It reads;

"To walk nightly as do the men-faeries we use not; but now and then we go together, and at good housewives' fires we wash our fairy children. If we find clean water and clean towels we leave them money, either in their basins, or in their shoes; but if we find no clean water in their houses, we wash our children in their pottage, milk, or beer, or whatever we find: for the sluts that have not such things fitting, we

[34] Keightley, Thomas, *The Fairy Mythology*, 227–228.
[35] Ibid., 296–297.

> wash their faces and hands with a gilded child's clout, or else carry them to some river and duck them over head and ears. We often use to dwell in some great hill, and from thence we do lend money to any poor man or woman that hath need; but if they bring it not again at the day appointed, we do not only punish them with pinching, but also in their goods, so that they never thrive till they have paid us."[36]

The tales tell us that their favorite offerings are cream, milk, white bread, and cheese.[37] The brownies were found in both England and in Scotland, North there as far as the Shetland Isles.[38]

[36] Ibid., 289.

[37] From a presentation given at Wic-can Fest - Paxson, Diana, "Lares and Landwights."

[38] Daniel Parkinson, "Boggart | Mysterious Britain & Ireland"; Arrowsmith, *A Field Guide to the Little People*, 193–196.

Bucca

The next faerie we'll talk about is the bucca. This faerie lives in the Cornwall section of England, which is found on the lower left side of the map above. I have seen two descriptions about this faerie, and I'm not fully sure which is correct.

In the book, "The Fairy-Faith in Celtic Countries," W.Y Evans-Wentz, a very well respected collector of folk lore, describes them as:

> "There was a very prevalent belief, when I was a boy, that this sea-strand pixy, called Bucca, had to be propitiated by a cast (three) of fish, to ensure the fishermen having a good shot (catch) of fish. The land pixy was supposed to be able to render its devotees invisible, if they only anointed their eyes with a certain green salve made of secret herbs gathered from Kerris-moor. In the invisible condition thus induced, people were able to join the pixy revels, during which, according to the old tradition, time slipped away very, very rapidly, though people returned from the pixies no older than when they went with them."[39]

And then in the book, "Popular Romances of the West of England: the Drolls, Traditions and Superstitions of Old Cornwall," Robert Hunt describes them as being the same as the knockers, which were the faeries that lived in caves and knocked on the walls to warn the miners of troubles.[40]

The book by Evan-Wentz came out in 1911, while the book by Hunt came out in 1903. In the Evan-Wentz book, he specifically says that Hunt had been in error with his description of the bucca.

---

[39] WY Evans-Wentz, *The Fairy-Faith in Celtic Countries*, 175.

[40] Robert Hunt, *Popular Romances of the West of England: The Drolls, Traditions and Superstitions of Old Cornwall 1903 - 3rd Edition* See - http://www.sacred-texts.com/neu/eng/prwe/prwe023.htm.

Evan-Wentz also believes that instead of being a faerie, the bucca is an early divinity and goes on to tell us that offerings were still being left for him by the sea in the town of Newlyn when his book was written. He backs this hypothesis up with a long discussion about how the name was derived, and compares it to the Welsh versions of a similar faerie.[41]

Overall, I tend to believe that this faerie really is a sea-side faerie, and not one found in the mines of Cornwall. Unfortunately, they do not figure in any of the fairy tales that I have found so far, so a better description will have to wait.

[41] WY Evans-Wentz, *The Fairy-Faith in Celtic Countries*, 165–166.

Churn Milk Peg & Melch Dick

Our next faerie is Churn Milk Peg. She is a nature faerie that comes to us from the folklore around Yorkshire, located in the upper middle section of the map above. It is said that she protects the hazelnut and oak trees and their crops, and would prevent anyone from taking them before they were ready. Because of this, she is also known as the Acorn Lady. Her name comes from the term for unripe hazel nuts, churn-milk nuts.[42]

In most of the stories about her, she is paired with another faerie called Melch Dick. He is said to be her male counterpart and together they guard the forests. Looking at the tales, they appear to travel around and are not connected with any one town.

One tale tells us that if anyone ate the nuts before they were ready, she would give them severe stomach cramps. And that she or Melch Dick would warn them first with a strong pinch! We also hear that both of them cannot abide laziness, and will bother anyone they catch lazing about beneath their trees.

Churn Milk Peg is also the name given to one of the standing stones in the town of Midgely, in Yorkshire County, near Hadrian's Wall.[43]

[42] Joseph Wright, *The English Dialect Dictionary: A-C - Google Books.*
[43] Ellen Phillips, *The Enchanted World: Fairies and Elves*, 50.

Duergar

The term duergar appears to come originally from the Germanic tribes, through the Anglo Saxons, then into modern English. It is described as being a type of dwarf, clothed in grey, and living underground. They are said to live in the North of England, near or above the border with Scotland.

Thomas Keightley, writing in the book, "The Fairy Mythology," describes them thus from the Germanic tales:

> "The Duergar are described as being of low stature, with short legs and long arms, reaching almost down to the ground when they stand erect. They are skilful and expert workmen in gold, silver, iron, and the other metals. They form many wonderful and extraordinary things for the Æser, and for mortal heroes, and the arms and armour that come from their forges are not to be paralleled."[44]

In the Eddas and Sagas, as well as being described as being formed from the maggot's in Ymir's flesh and therefore burrowing under the ground, they are the dwarfs that made the golden hair for Sif, and many of the other wondrous tools used by the Old Gods.

There is a story told in the North of England about a traveler in the mountains who came upon a stone hut with a dying fire in front of it. As he sat by it, a duergar walked out of the forest and joined him. The duergar picked up a log, broke it over his knee and put it on the fire. Towards morning, the duergar invited the man to put another log on. He refused and sat still. At first light, the duergar vanished along with the hut, and the man found himself sitting next to a cliff. If he had moved to get a log, he would have fallen over the cliff and died.[45]

[44] Keightley, Thomas, *The Fairy Mythology*, 67.
[45] Larkin, *Faeries.*

Hobgoblin

Moving on, we come to the hobgoblin. It is thought by some folklorist, that the term hobgoblin is derived from Robin Goblin, an early character in the tales. Today, the fairy known as Robin Goodfellow is also likely derived from this same character. Many of the descriptions of the hobgoblin that people are most familiar with come from modern literature, for example Tolkien's work, the Spiderwick Chronicles, and many of the role-playing games.

We do find examples in the folktales, as well as the modern ones. In there, we find that the hobgoblins like to stay in houses sitting by the hob, where they can be warm and dry. Hob is an interesting word, and I wasn't familiar with it myself. According to the dictionary, it means, "a projection at the back or side of a fireplace on which something may be kept warm."[46]

They were usually described as being about one to two feet high, and dressed in brown clothes. They were not harmful beings, and would help with chores and other things. In days past, there were many hobgoblins that had lived in the same house long enough to be known by name. Some of those names that have come down to us include "Hob-Gob, Tom-Tit, Robin Round Cap, Hob-thrush Hob, and Goblin Groom." Unfortunately, sightings have become rare, and many people think that the hobgoblins have gone elsewhere.[47]

46 "Hob - Definition and More from the Free Merriam-Webster Dictionary."

47 Arrowsmith, *A Field Guide to the Little People*, 120.

Jack In Irons

Jack In Irons is a giant that can be found in the Yorkshire area, found in the upper middle area on the map above. It is said that he is covered with rusted chains, from where people have tried to trap him, and that he attaches the heads of his victims to those chains. He is also known to carry a large spiked club.

Unfortunately, not much more is known about him.[48]

[48] Larkin, *Faeries.*

Jenny Greenteeth

Next, we have Jenny Greenteeth, not a pretty name by any means. She is also known as Ginny Greenteeth, Wicked Jenny, or Peg o' Nell. She is a river hag that is known for pulling children into the river to drown them.

Tales of her are common in the Lancashire area, as well as the areas around Cheshire and Shropshire in the Northeast of England, about the middle left of the map above. She is often described as green-skinned, with long hair, and sharp teeth. Many folklorists believe that she was an invented tale to keep children away from the rivers and other bodies of water, and I'm sure it probably worked well!

It is interesting to see that this name is also used to describe the pondweed that covers the surface of small ponds, and this may have been the origin of the legend, owing to the fact that it is easy to get tangled in weeds and drown.

Charles Hardwick, writing in 1872, talks about her in the book, "Traditions Superstitions and Folklore of Lancaster and the North of England." He says:

> "I remember well, when very young, being cautioned against approaching to the side of stagnant pools of water partially covered with vegetation. At One time, I firmly believed that, if I disobeyed this instruction, a certain water 'boggart' named 'Jenny Greenteeth' would drag me beneath her verdant screen and subject me to other tortures besides death by drowning."[49]

[49] Charles Hardwick, *Traditions Superstitions and Folklore of Lancaster and the North of England*, 279.

Knockers

In the tin mines of the Devon and Cornwall area of England, lower left end of the map above, we find our next faerie, the knockers.

They are beneficial faeries and will "knock" on the walls to lead miners to veins of tin. They are also said to warn miners of impending cave-ins. To keep them on the good side, miners would leave small amounts of their afternoon meal, traditionally called a "pastie." People say that the knockers are still active today, and if you try to explore the mines, you may hear them.

We hear about them in Robert Hunt's book, "Popular Romances of the West of England: the Drolls, Traditions and Superstitions of Old Cornwall." There he tells us:

> "An old man and his son, called Trenwith, who lived near Bosprenis, went out one Midsummer Eve, about midnight, and watched until they saw the 'Smae People' bringing up the shining ore. It is said they were possessed of some secret by which they could communicate with the fairy people. Be this as it may, they told the little miners that they would save them all the trouble of breaking down the ore, that they would bring 'to grass' for them, one-tenth of the 'richest stuff,' and leave it properly dressed, if they would quietly give them up this end. An agreement of some kind was come to. The old man and his son took the 'pitch,' and in a short time realised much wealth. The old man never failed to keep to his bargain, and leave the tenth of the ore for his friends. He died. The son was avaricious and selfish. He sought to cheat the Knockers, but he ruined himself by so doing."[50]

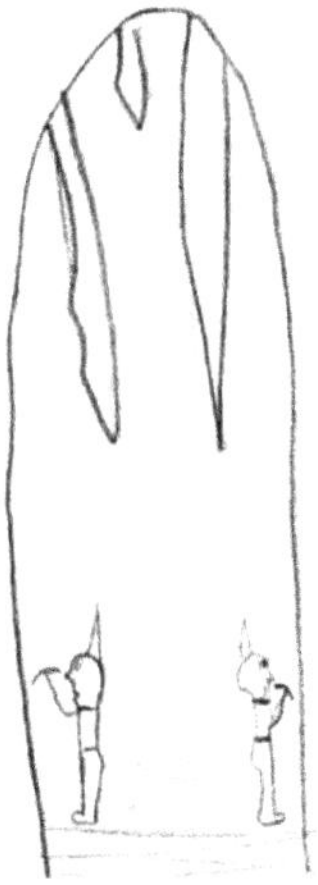

[50] Robert Hunt, *Popular Romances of the West of England: The Drolls, Traditions and Superstitions of Old Cornwall 1903 - 3rd Edition.*

Morgan

Our next faerie is called the Morgan, and is a sea-fairy, or mermaid found on the Cornwall coasts. She is very similar to the Breton faerie of the same name, which isn't too strange since Cornwall and Brittany are just over the English Channel from each other. Other names for these faerie, when referring to the race as a whole, are the *Morveth*, which means sea-daughters in Breton, or merry-maids as used by the Cornish fishermen

There are tales told along the sea coasts of women being seen spending time on the rocks watching the sea and weeping, or of small groups of women going to peculiar isolated rocks at special seasons. Perhaps, these were faeries trapped on shore, as in the stories told of the Irish *roanes*, or the Scottish *selkies*?

It was said that in the parish of Zennor on the coast, there was a carving of a mermaid on one of the benches that people "thought strange to be in a church."[51] One of the stories that talks about this is called "The Mermaid of Zennor," and I've included a small section here.

> "Hundreds of years ago a very beautiful and richly attired lady attended service in Zennor Church occasionally—now and then she went to Morvah also;—her visits were by no means regular,—often long intervals would elapse between them.
> Yet whenever she came the people were enchanted with her good looks and sweet singing. Although Zennor folks were remarkable for their fine psalmody, she excelled them all; and they wondered how, after the scores of years that they had seen her, she continued to look so young and fair. No one knew whence she came nor whither she went; yet many watched her as far as they could see from Tregarthen Hill.

[51] Ibid. See http://www.sacred-texts.com/neu/eng/prwe/prwe058.htm.

She took some notice of a fine young man, called Mathey Trewella, who was the best singer in the parish. He once followed her, but he never returned; after that she was never more seen in Zennor Church, and it might not have been known to this day who or what she was but for the merest accident.

One Sunday morning a vessel cast anchor about a mile from Pendower Cove; soon after a mermaid came close alongside and hailed the ship. Rising out of the water as far as her waist, with her yellow hair floating around her, she told the captain that she was returning from church, and requested him to trip his anchor just for a minute, as the fluke of it rested on the door of her dwelling, and she was anxious to get in to her children.

When Zennor folks learnt that a mermaid dwelt near Pendower, and what she had told the captain, they concluded it was this sea-lady who had visited their church, and enticed Trewella to her abode. To commemorate these somewhat unusual events they had the figure she bore—when in her ocean-home—carved in holy-oak, which may still be seen."[52]

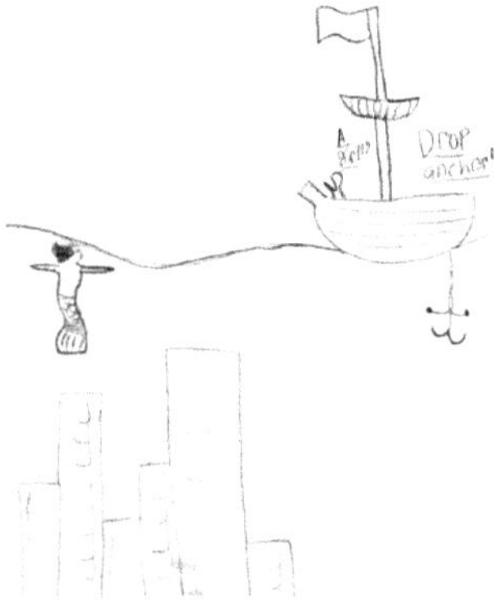

The sightings of mermaids occur all along the shores in this area, not only in Cornwall and Brittany, but up along the Welsh coasts as well. I'll be talking more about the stories for Wales in the chapter for that country.

[52] William Bottrell, *Traditions and Hearthside Stories of West Cornwall, Vol. 2* See http://www.sacred-texts.com/neu/celt/swc2/swc274.htm.

Nanny Button Cap

Our next faerie is one of the nursery faeries. The stories about her come from the Yorkshire section of England, which is in the upper middle area of the map above. She checks on the children and makes sure they are safe and warm in bed. Other than that, not much is known, and I haven't found any references to her in the folk tales.

We do have one poem that has come down to us, and it is found in the book, "Yorkshire Dialect Poems," written in the early 1900's by F.W. Moorman. It reads:

"T' moon shines breet,
T' stars give leet,
An' little Nanny Button-cap
Will coom to-morra neet."[53]

[53] F.W. Moorman, "Yorkshire Dialect Poems."

Oakmen

All over England, there are remains of groves of trees that were sacred to the Druids. It is said that in these groves live a type of faerie called the oakmen. They especially like areas where the English Oaks saplings grow up from old trunks. They are described as being dwarf-like creatures that dislike mankind, for the destruction they have done to the trees, but protect the animals of trees of the forest.

It is said that a sure sign the oakmen are in the area, is if bluebells are growing up around the oak stumps. While tales of these faeries may represent actual sightings, they may also represent stories of the ancient Druids that that have been kept alive by the local people.[54]

[54] Ellen Phillips, *The Enchanted World: Fairies and Elves*, 52; "Oakmen."

One With the White Hand

Our next faerie is found on the moors of Somerset, located near the bottom left side on the map above. This is a faerie that lives in the groves of birch trees, and is another of the unfriendly faeries. It is said that she lies in wait for unwary travelers, and if she touches them on the head, then they will go mad; but if she can touch them on the chest, then they will die. She is usually described as being female, pale in color and skinny to the point where all of her ribs are showing.[55]

As we have, and will continue to see, there are many unfriendly faeries described by people living in a pre-technological period. For them, the woods and fields were a scary place at night, and that's when most of the faerie sightings occurred. Anyone who has walked in the forest by torchlight, and I mean a real torch not a flashlight, knows that the shadows do strange things to the imagination.

[55] Ellen Phillips, *The Enchanted World: Fairies and Elves*, 53.

Pillywiggin

Our next faerie is one of the flower faeries. These faeries remind me of the "Disney" type of faeries, more than any of the other faeries from the tales. It is usually found living in the flowers of plants, and it is said that each type of plant has its own kind of flower faerie. In England, they are found living in all areas. The notable plants, each said to have a faerie watching over it, were the wildflowers — like bluebells, foxglove, cowslips and other plants that produced large, showy flowers.

Modern tales tell us that these faeries resembled humans, but with insect-like wings and antenna. They are said to live in family groups, again like the Tinkerbelle movies, and protect the plants. It is also said that they can be dangerous if you try to harm the plants, and can sting like a bee!

Because they are so well known, they are used as characters in many children's books, and have even made it into the videogame Final Fantasy XI.[56]

[56] Ibid, 56; Pillywiggins Garden, "Pilly...What? - Pillywiggins Garden"; "wikipedia.org/wiki/Pillywiggin - French Edition."

Pixie

Another type of faerie that many are familiar with from the Harry Potter films is the pixie, also known as the piskies, or piscy. The stories about them are mostly from the southwest part of England, around the counties of Cornwall and Devon, found on the bottom left part of the map above. Similar types of faeries are found throughout the areas described in this book under different names.

Usually they are seen as good-hearted creatures with a love of good pranks. In many of the stories, they are not trying to kill the humans involved, just "bother them greatly." They respond better to children and older people than they do to teens and younger adults. For this latter group, they will many times lead them off into the moors to be "lost for a bit."

They are usually described as being old men, with wrinkled skin and red hair. They are usually less than a foot in height, and are depicted as dressing in earth-tone colors, especially green, using natural materials. In some of the cases, they appear to people as bundles of rags.

In the wilder areas around Cornwall, there are many lonely places with ancient stones on them, which are said to be the homes of the pixies. Reading the description of faeries in the play, "A Midsummer Night's Dream," I feel that these are the ones that Shakespeare was talking about.

The pixies were so prevalent, that many clergymen became famous for their "charms against the pixies." One charm that comes down to us reads:

> "No Pigsey could harm a man if his coat were inside-out, and it became a very common practice for persons who had to go from village to village by night, to wear their jacket or cloak so turned, ostensibly to prevent the dew from taking the shine off the cloth, but in reality to render them safe from the Pigseys."[57]

[57] Robert Hunt, *Popular Romances of the West of England: The Drolls, Traditions and Superstitions of Old Cornwall 1903 - 3rd Edition* See http://www.sacred-texts.com/neu/eng/prwe/prwe023.htm; MacKillop, *Dictionary of Celtic Mythology*, 324.

The pixies are said to be very fond of music, and in the evenings will sit in the faerie rings to play and dance. Any humans that join them may find that time moves different inside the rings, and may be gone longer than they thought. Their music may not sound traditional to modern folks, but according to the tales, the sounds of nature was the music. Whether it was the croaking of frog, the chip of crickets, or the cry of the owl, it was all blended into the music they made. The pixies are said to be fond of mirth and laughter as well, and a common saying in the Cornwall area is "to laugh like a piskie."

Unlike the flower faeries living in plants, the pixies were said to build houses in the woods. One description has come down to us in the tales. It reads:

> "A Pixy-house is often said to be in a rock; sometimes, however, a mole hill is a palace for the elves, or a hollow nut cracked by the 'joiner squirrel,' will contain the majesty of Pixy-land. And Drayton, who wrote of these little fanciful beings as if he were the chosen laureate of their race, thus describes their royal dwelling.
> 'The walls of spiders' legs are made, well morticed and finely laid, he was the master of his trade. It curiously that builded; the windows of the eyes of cats, and for a roof, instead of slats, is covered with the skins of bats, with moonshine that are gilded.'"[58]

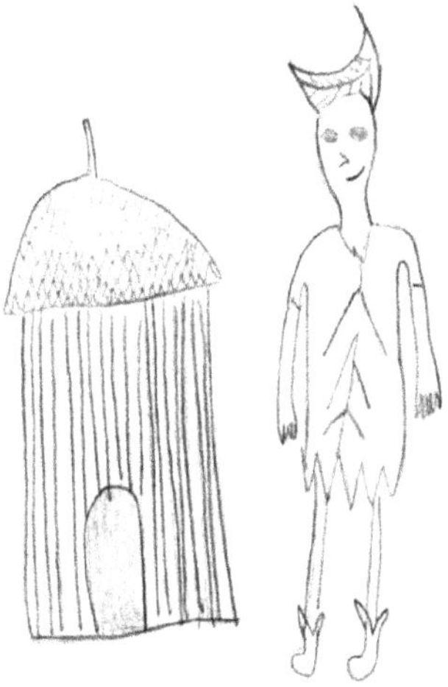

[58] Anna Eliza Bray, *A Peep at the Pixies, or Legends of the West* See http://www.sacred-texts.com/neu/eng/ppx/ppx03.htm.

Portunes

Our next type of faeries are the portunes. They can be very helpful to human kind **most of the time**, and then turn around and be bothersome. Usually, they help out on farms with the chores, such as clean up, haying, tilling, or any other work they can do at night, while the family is sleeping. They are said to resemble small old men who stand less than an inch high.

Since the Romans occupied much of England, you have to wonder if their name had anything to do with the Roman God of doors, keys and livestock, who was also called Portunes? All of the stories that have come down to us are from long after the Roman occupation, so it is a definite possibility and seems to work in with the God's concerns with farms and livestock.

Our best references to the English portunes are from Thomas Keightley, writing in 1870 in the book, "The Fairy Mythology." In it, he tells us:

> "It is their nature to embrace the simple life of comfortable farmers, and when, on account of their domestic work, they are sitting up at night, when the doors are shut, they warm themselves at the fire, and take little frogs out of their bosom, roast them on the coals, and eat them."

He then goes on to tell us about their one "bad" habit.

> "[When]the English are riding anywhere alone, the Portune sometimes invisibly joins the horseman; and when he has accompanied him a good while, he at last takes the reins, and leads the horse into a neighbouring slough; and when he is fixed and floundering in it, the Portune goes off with a loud laugh..."[59]

[59] Keightley, Thomas, *The Fairy Mythology*, 286.

Spriggans

Our next faerie race is the spriggans. The spriggans are a group of faeries living in the Cornwall area of England, near the bottom left of the map above. They are like the pixies, but the spriggans are more spiteful and full of malice. Where the pixies will play trick that are not really harmful, the spriggans love to do tricks that hurt, or even kill humans.

It was believed that the spriggans haunted the lonely places such as ruins, certain standing stones, barrows, and windswept crags. They were thought to be descended from the trolls, and were often found near where giants were active.

It is also said that they want to steal small children, and replace them with their own kind. If you have seen the movie "Labyrinth," the spriggans are the ones that took the baby for the Fairy King. In appearance, the spriggans are described as grotesquely ugly with wizened features and crooked skinny bodies.

We get a good description from them in the book, "Popular Romances of the West of England," edited and collected by Robert Hunt in 1881. There he writes:

> "This is known, that they were a remarkably mischievous arid thievish tribe. If ever a house was robbed, a child stolen, cattle carried away, or a building demolished, it was the work of the Spriggans. Whatever commotion took place in earth, air, or water, it was all put down as the work of these spirits. … It is usually considered that they are the ghosts of the giants; certainly, from many of their feats, we must suppose them to possess giant's strength. The Spriggans have the charge of buried treasure."[60]

[60] Robert Hunt, *Popular Romances of the West of England: The Drolls, Traditions and Superstitions of Old Cornwall 1903 - 3rd Edition* See http://www.sacred-texts.com/neu/eng/prwe/prwe023.htm.

Tatter-Foal

Our next faerie is from the Lincolnshire area of England, on the middle right of the map above, and is called either the tatter-foal, or the shag-foal. It appears to travelers in the night as a shaggy looking horse, and when it comes near to them it will pull them out of the saddle, or scare off their horse and make them fall off. It has also been said to ride up close behind them and then "mount" their horse and try to squeeze them to death with its front legs.

Local legends say that it was the spirit of a person that had been hung near where it appeared, but the appearances happened near four of five different villages, so this seems unlikely. One of the sighting descriptions may give a further explanation, especially the drinking part in italics.

> "Why, he is a shagg'd-looking hoss, and given to all manner of goings-on, fra cluzzening hold of a body what is riding home *half-screwed with bargain drink*, and pulling him out of the saddle, to scaring a old woman three parts out of her skin, and making her drop her shop-things in the blatter and blash, and run for it."[61]

[61] Eliza Gutch and M. G. W. Peacock, *Examples of Printed Folk-Lore Concerning Lincolnshire*, 5:55–56.

Thrummy Caps

Our next faeries are the thrummy caps. These faeries are credited with the high quality of wool in the northern counties of England, near Northumberland, which is in the upper center of the map above. Their name came from the fact that they wore caps made of thrums.

Thrum is another interesting word, and another one I didn't know, so I had to look it up. The definition states that it is the excess wool clipped off when weaving is done.[62] Some accounts state that they live in the cellars of old, abandoned houses, but others state that they live in the Thrummy Hills of North Yorkshire, which is two counties south of Northumberland.[63]

62 "Thrum - Definition and More from the Free Merriam-Webster Dictionary."
63 WY Evans-Wentz, *The Fairy-Faith in Celtic Countries*, 395.

Will-o-the-Wisp

On lonely section of the moors, glowing lights that move and dance in front of you are sometimes seen. These are the will-o-the-wisps. This is a common phenomenon throughout the British Isles, and are known by many names. Here are just a few of the many regional names it is known by, just within England.

- Hertfordshire and East Anglia: The Hobby Lantern
- Lancashire: Peg-a-Lantern
- Cornwall: and Somerset: Joan the Wad
- East Anglia: The Lantern Man
- Somerset and Devon: Hinky Punk
- Shropshire: Will the Smith
- Worcestershire: Pinket
- The West Country: Jacky Lantern, Jack a Lantern
- Norfolk: Will o the Wikes
- Warwickshire Gloucestershire: Hobbedy's Lantern
- North Yorkshire, Northumberland: Jenny with the Lantern

It is generally believed that they are solitary faeries who delight in taking a traveler out of their way and getting them lost. Although they not seen as being too dangerous, they can be very annoying. At times though, the traveler is taken to a dangerous spot, for example in a marsh, or on the edge of a cliff and then left to their own to get out of, or off it after the lights go out.

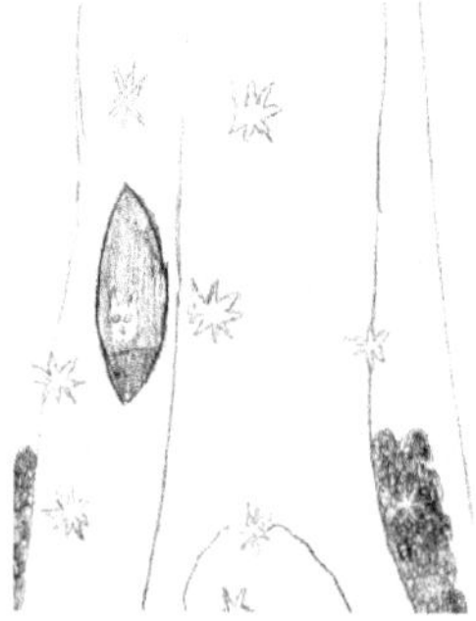

The lights were also seen as death omens, and when seen within graveyards, they were known as corpse lights. These were said to light the path of a coming funeral — from the victims' home to the graveyard — in the form of small flickering flames. In other tales the light were often said to appear in places where a tragedy was about to occur.[64]

[64] Arrowsmith, *A Field Guide to the Little People*, 34–36 and many others.

4 IRELAND[65]

[65] "Irish_map_ireland_counties_green.gif."

Alp-Luachra

We start our chapter on Ireland with one of the solitary faeries. They are the *alp-luachra*, or joint eaters. This faerie is also called *alt-pluachra* in one of the tales. The tales tell us that if you are alone in the woods and fall asleep by a stream, the *alp-luachra* might find you. If it does, it is said that they will take the form of a newt or salamander and crawl into your mouth to steal the "essence" of the food you have eaten.

One of the tales tells of a man who lay down in a field next to a stream while his men were harvesting the grain. When he woke up, he felt strange and over time, he started feeling worse and called for the doctors to find out what was wrong with him. Nothing they did helped.

About a year later, a holy man came by and saw that he was sick, and on questioning him about his illness, knew that he had swallowed a *alp-luachra*. He sent him to Mac Dermott, the Prince of Coolavin. When he told the prince his story, the prince knew just what to do. He had the man eat a large meal of salt pork, then lie down over a stream with his mouth open above the water.

He told the man not to move no matter what happened, then went back a few feet to leave him alone. After a bit of time, first one, then a total of twelve small newts came out of his mouth and jumped into the water.

Seeing more than one *alp-luachra* jump out, the prince knew that the man had first swallowed an adult faerie, which over the time had given birth to a litter of young. It was only the young ones that had come out so far, so he told the man to wait longer for the mother to come out. At last, she did come out and jumped into the water with her children. The man couldn't thank the prince enough, and slowly started gaining back all of the weight he had lost.[66]

[66] Douglas Hyde, *Beside The Fire: A Collection of Irish Gaelic Folk Stories*, 47–74.; MacKillop, *Dictionary of Celtic Mythology*, 12.

Banshee

Our next faerie is one of the best known of all the faeries. She is the *banshee* and is found all over Ireland and Scotland. The term *banshee* comes from the Old Irish, *bean sídhe*, which means woman of the *sídhe*, or woman of the fairy mounds. She is usually seen as an omen of death or a messenger from the Otherworld. The tales that talk about *banshees* are too numerous to count, but most of them agree in just what role the banshee plays in Irish life.

Usually a *banshee* would be connected to an individual family, and when they heard her wail, they knew that someone in their family would die. In many of the tales, distance to the person who has died had no effect. For example, there are tales of people who had immigrated to America or Canada dying, and their families back in Ireland would know about it when the family *banshee* wailed.

While in some of the tales, the *banshee* is never see, other tales tell of seeing just a face or head of a woman floating above the ground. Some descriptions talk of the *banshees* dressed in white or grey, and often having long, fair hair, which they brush with a silver comb. Other stories portray *banshees* as dressed in green, red, or black, with a grey cloak. Almost every time that the *banshee* is seen, their dress is said to be of "an old style," as was worn many years ago.[67]

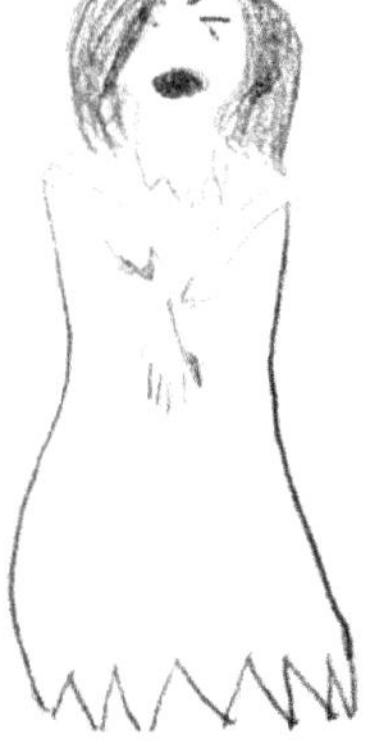

[67] WB Yeats, *Fairy and Folk Tales of the Irish Peasantry*, 171; Thomas Crofton Croker, *Fairy Legends and Traditions of the South of Ireland*, 151–152 and many others.

Bean-tighe

For our next faerie, we talk about the *bean-tighe*, which is a faerie housekeeper. The word literally means "woman of the house" in Irish. They were believed to look like old women, dressed in old fashion peasant clothes, and would finish any cleaning not done in the house during the night, or when the people were away. They are very friendly to humans, and wished to have a friendly human house to watch over.

It was also believe that they would look after the children in the house and take care of them during the night to keep away the bad dreams. It is thought that they love fresh strawberries and cream, and if you are willing to give this to them, and allow them to live with you, they are easy to keep happy and **very** helpful.

It is interesting that old women living in Ireland in olden times had to be careful not to keep too clean a house, as they would be accused of having a fairy living with them and be subject to prosecution from the churchmen.[68]

[68] WY Evans-Wentz, *The Fairy-Faith in Celtic Countries*, 81–82; Larkin, *Faeries.*

Boggart

Our next fairy group of faeries are the *boggarts*. The Irish *boggarts* are very similar to the English *boggarts* and many of the tales about them could be written about either of them. Both of these faeries are very similar to the Scottish *brownies*, which I'll be talking about in the chapter on Scotland.

Like their counterparts, these faeries are usually depicted as being mischievous, but as long as they are treated kindly, will not be too much of a problem. There is one tale though that talks about a family with a young boy in it that likes to stick things into a hole in the wall that was called the "Boggart's Hole." The *boggart* definitely did not like this behavior and made it a practice that whatever had been stuck in the hole would be thrown back out at a high rate of speed to strike the person who had put it in.

Over time, and the nursing of many bruises, the family learned not to put anything into the boggart's hole.[69]

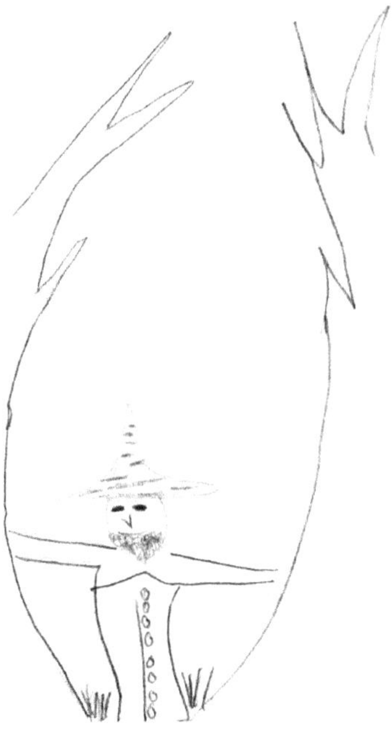

[69] Thomas Crofton Croker, *Fairy Legends and Traditions of the South of Ireland*, 109–110.

Buachailleen

The *buachailleen* are Irish water faeries, also known as the Herding Boys. Their favorite haunts are in streams in the pastures where cattle are kept during the summers. Their name of the herding boys comes from their love of mixing with the cattle and moving them to places where the herders are not expecting them.

Like many of the solitary faeries, they are known to be great shape shifters, and can easily fool the herders into thinking they are just other cattle. When they appeared in human shape, they were usually seen as small boys, and many reports have them wearing small red hats, that may have been made of flower petals, or flower heads.

Along with moving the cattle, there are other stories of the *buachailleen* tormenting the herd boys by throwing rocks at them, or making sounds in the night to scare them.[70]

[70] WY Evans-Wentz, *The Fairy-Faith in Celtic Countries*, 81.

Cluricaune

Our next Irish faerie, the *cluricaune*, is one that is often confused with the *leprechaun*. They both like solitude, are similar in appearance, and are considered keepers of treasure, but the *cluricaune* is more willing to interact with people.

A good description of this type of faerie is found in the book "Fairy Legends and Traditions of the South of Ireland," in the tale of "The Haunted Cellar." The description reads:

> "Mac Carthy contemplated the little fellow with wonder. He wore a red night-cap on his head; before him was a short leather apron, which now, from his attitude, fell rather on one side; and he had stockings of a light blue colour, so long as nearly to cover the entire of his leg; with shoes, having huge silver buckles in them, and with high heels (perhaps out of vanity to make him appear taller). His face was like a withered winter apple; and his nose, which was of a bright crimson colour, about the tip wore a delicate purple bloom, like that of a plum; yet his eyes twinkled 'like those mites of candied dew in moony nights' and his mouth twitched up at one side with an arch grin."[71]

It's easy to see that described as wearing a leather apron, being short, and having a cap upon his head, all sound like a description that could be describing a *leprechaun*, but in this story, he calls himself "your *cluricaune* Naggeneen." It is said that the *cluricaunes* love a small drink left out for them, and are usually seen smoking a *dudeen*, a short pipe. These pipes are often dug up in the countryside, and when found are taken for evidence that the faeries live nearby.

---

[71] Thomas Crofton Croker, *Fairy Legends and Traditions of the South of Ireland*, 105.

The *cluricaune* is said to usually carry a leather "purse" which contains a magic shilling, and no matter how many time he spends it, it always comes back to the purse. Other tales say that he carries two purses, one with the magic shilling, and another with a brass coin that he gives to people who catch him, in exchange for the real magic coin.[72]

[72] Ibid, 115.

Dullahan

Moving on, we come to the *dullahan*. The name may also be seen as *dulachan* (in Irish *dubhlachan*), or *durrachan*. The *dullahan* is described in two different ways. They are talked about as either riding a black horse, which is sometimes headless itself, or of driving a black carriage, pulled by headless horses. In both cases, the *dullahan* is headless themselves, and are usually carrying their head under their arm. An interesting thing is that all of the tales talk about how they make no noise as they pass by on a road.

Some of the tales talk about how when he is driving a carriage or wagon, the wagon has skulls with candles in them for headlights, and wheels made out of bones. It is thought that the *dullahan's* job is to take the people as they die to the Otherworld, like the *ankou* in Brittany.

It is **VERY** bad luck to see the *dullahan*, and it is even said that if you do see him, you will be the next one he comes for. When the *dullahan* stops riding, that is where a person due to die is located. The *dullahan* will then call out their name, and they immediately die. It is also said that you can't hide from the *dullahan*, and when it is your time, he will find you wherever you are.[73]

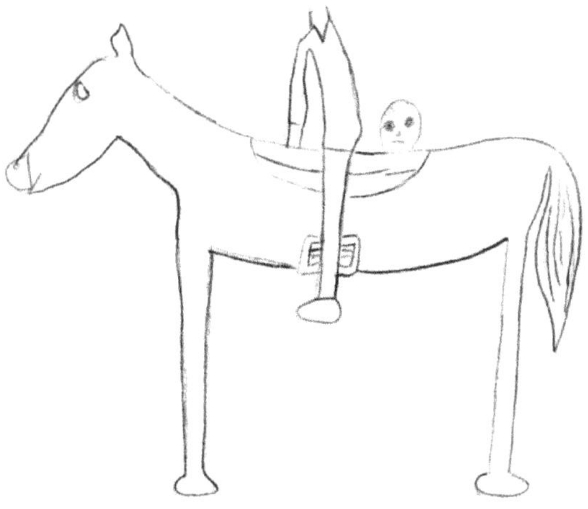

[73] Ibid, 317–320.

Each Uisce

Our next faerie is the *each uisce,* which is an Irish water horse. It is similar to the Scottish faerie called the *each uisge*. Both though are different from the Scottish *kelpie,* who also takes the shape of a horse. The *kelpie* is only found in running water, while the *each uisce* and the *each uisge* are found in either salt water, lakes or bogs. We'll talk more about the Scottish faeries in the chapter on Scotland.

The tales all describe this faerie as appearing as a beautiful looking horse, which appears so tame it is almost begging to be handled and ridden. Once a person got on though, the animal's demeanor changed and the person is given a wild ride until he is taken into the sea or lake where the faerie would drown and devourer him. The tales tell about how the person would disappear completely, except for the liver with the *each uisce* did not like to eat. The liver would float to the surface of the sea or lake, so the other people would know what had happened to their friend.[74]

[74] MacKillop, *Dictionary of Celtic Mythology*, 145.

Féar Dearg

Now we come to the *féar dearg,* which means "red man." He was, and some say, still is the practical joker of the faerie realm. As one of the solitary faeries, he prefers to work alone. In the tales, he always dressed in red and played many tricks upon unsuspecting mortals. Sometimes he would come in to warm himself by a person's fire, and if the people of the house raised no objections to him they prospered; but if they said any words against him, bad luck happened to that person.

It is told that these faeries are attached to the location, or house, rather than to the family that lives there. This is unlike the *cluricaun* who is attached to the family, and is willing to move with them.

One of the tales tell about a man coming upon a whole group of *féar dearg* who were getting ready to go to battle with another group. The leader of the troop said that he needed a horse to take him there, and jumping upon the man's back, turned him into the horse. After the battle was over, the *féar dearg* turned him back into a human again.[75]

[75] Thomas Crofton Croker, *Fairy Legends and Traditions of the South of Ireland*, 357–358, 360, 389, 395–396. See also "The Pooka of Murroe & Fear Dearg (Red Man)" - http://www.sacred-texts.com/neu/celt/lfic/lfic029.htm.

Féar Gurtha

Our next fairy type is the *féar gurtha*, which means "The Hungry Grass." This legend appears to have started after the Great Famine of 1848. Stories appeared about certain patches of land that were bewitched. It was said that if a traveler passed over them, he would suffer uncontrollable pangs of hunger and if assistance were not given to him immediately, he would die right there on the ground. Irish peasants used to sprinkle the grass with any leftover crumbs from their meals, in order to stave off the *féar gurtha*. This was supposedly sent as a warning from the faeries against the people's lack of generosity. This tale was first told by William Carleton, in The Dublin University Magazine for April 1856. It was called "*Fair Gurtha*, or the Hungry-Grass."[76]

There was also a f*éar gurtha* or "hungry man," who appeared as a travelling merchant. He was said to be a gaunt figure, miserably clad who begged alms from passers-by. Those giving alms received good fortune for the rest of their lives, while those refusing suffered some calamity, whereby they were reduced to poverty themselves and knew the gnawing pangs of hunger.

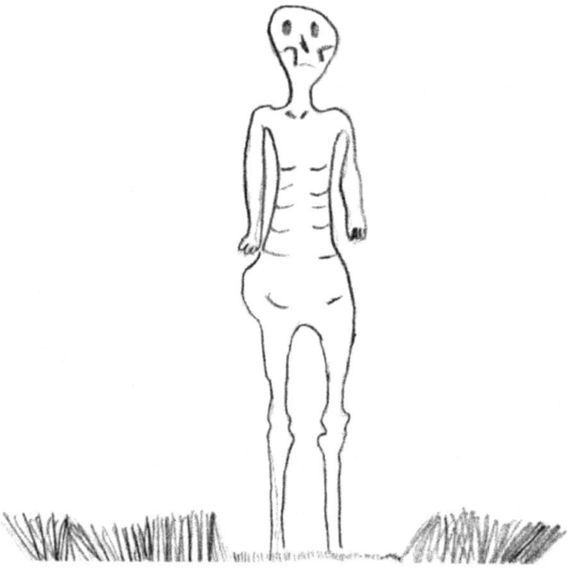

[76] REV. JOHN O'HANLON, *Fairy Beliefs - Irish Folklore.*

Geancanach

Moving on, we come to the *geancanach*. They are another solitary faerie, who is described as being pixie-like in appearance, with big slanted eyes, and large pointed ears. They are usually described as being small, no more than a few inches in height, and having nice, playful smiles. They have wings, but move so fast, it is as if they teleport from place to place.

Another tale describes him as the love-talker. It tells how he strolls about the countryside with his hands in his pockets and a *dudeen*, a short Irish pipe, in his mouth, "gostering" with the idle boys." Gostering is another interesting word, and it means "to boastfully talk." To meet him meant bad luck, and whoever was ruined by ill-judged love, was said to have been with the *geancanach*.[77] It was also said that they would die soon. Talking about this, one Irish saying reads:

> "Who meets the Love talker, must weave her shroud soon."[78]

[77] Alfred Perceval Graves, *The Irish Fairy Book*, xii.

[78] Ellen Phillips, *The Enchanted World: Fairies and Elves*, 112.

Leanan-Sídhe

If we think of the *banshee* as the portent of death, then we should think of our next faerie, the *leanan-sídhe* as the call of life. She is the inspirer of poets and writers, the faerie who brings inspiration into the soul of the people. She is also the faerie lover, who feeds on the love and affection of humans. You may also see this written as *leannán-sídhe* or *báinleannán*. It is from the Irish *báine*, meaning "white or pale," and *leannán*, meaning "lover."[79] It is said that once she starts to inspire a human, they will waste away and die if she leaves them, unless they can find another faerie to attract.

Lady Francesca Speranza Wilde, writing in the book "Ancient Legends, Mystic Charms, and Superstitions of Ireland" tells us about a time when the king of Ireland was depressed and called for one of his poets to inspire him. She came to him and the power of the *leanan-sídhe* was in her. The passage reads:

> "So Eodain [the poet] came to him, and upheld him with her strong spirit, for she had the power within her of the poet and the prophet, and she said--
> 'Arise now, O king, and govern like a true hero, and bring confusion on the evil workers. Be strong and fear not, for by strength and justice kings should rule.'
> And Eugene the king was guided by her counsel and was successful. And he overthrew his enemies and brought back peace and order to the land. For the strength of the Leanan Sidhe was in the words of Eodain, the power of the spirit of life which is given to the poet and the prophet, by which they inspire and guide the hearts of men."[80]

---

[79] MacKillop, *Dictionary of Celtic Mythology*, 28.

[80] Lady Francesca Speranza Wilde, *Ancient Legends, Mystic Charms, and Superstitions of Ireland* See also - http://www.sacred-texts.com/neu/celt/ali/ali071.htm.

There are many other writers and poets among the Irish people who had a close relationship with this fairy and who were inspired by her. Some people say that the great Irish writer and poet William Butler (WB) Yeats was inspired by his "faerie" connection. In the introduction to his book, "Irish Fairy Tales," he tells us:

> "Do you think the Irish peasant would be so full of poetry if he had not his faeries? Do you think the peasant girls of Donegal, when they are going to service inland, would kneel down as they do and kiss the sea with their lips if both sea and land were not made lovable to them by beautiful legends and wild sad stories?"[81]

[81] WB Yeats, *Irish Fairy Tales - Yeats 1892*, 6.

Leprechaun

Our next faerie type is the *leprechaun*. I'm sure that everyone knows about this type. He is the fairy shoemaker in the tales, with the large pipe in his mouth. He is the keeper of the pot of gold that he hides from everyone, but which he will give to you, **IF** you can catch him! Most of us know the secret to catching him, and that is to keep your eyes on him. If you blink for even a second, he will disappear on you.

In most tales and stories, *leprechauns* are depicted as generally harmless creatures who enjoy solitude and live in remote locations, although opinion is divided as to if they ever enjoy the company of other spirits. Although rarely seen in social situations, *leprechauns* are supposedly very well spoken and, if ever spoken to, could make good conversation. By nature, *leprechauns* are said to be ill natured and mischievous, with a mind for cunning. Many tales show the *leprechaun* outwitting a human, or a group of humans.[82]

[82] MacKillop, *Dictionary of Celtic Mythology*, 263 and many, many others.

Lunantishee

Moving on, we have the *lunantishee*. They are a tribe of faeries who guard the blackthorn trees. They will not allow a blackthorn stick to be cut on Beltaine (May Eve) or Samhain (November Eve). Should anyone manage to cut a stick on one of those days, it is said that something bad will surely happen to them[83].

They are described as appearing as wizened old bald men, with pointed long teeth and long arms and fingers. It is also said that they are said to leave their trees only to dance in the moonlight, and also that they dislike humans, who only seem to want to cut down their trees.

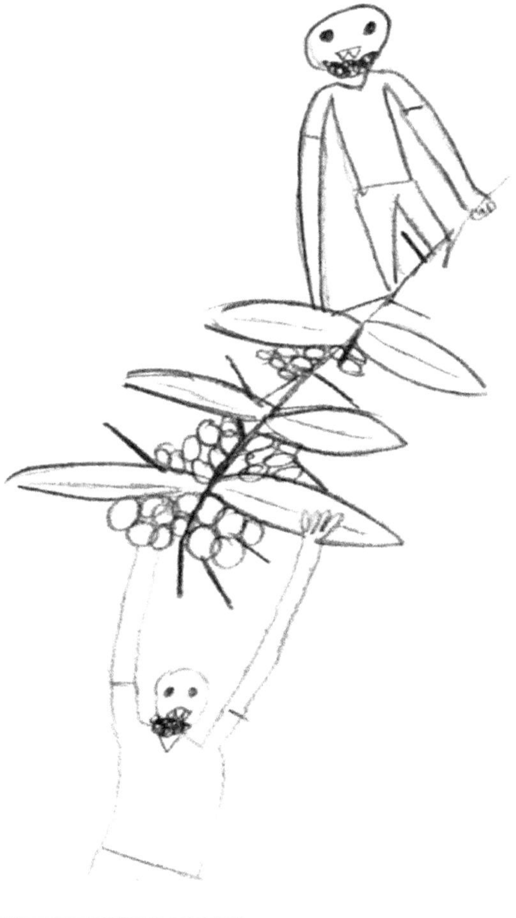

[83] WY Evans-Wentz, *The Fairy-Faith in Celtic Countries*, 52–53.

Maighdean-mhara (Sea-Maiden)

The *maighdean-mhara* are the sea-maids, or sea-people that inhabit the coasts of Ireland. In Irish, they are also called *moruadh* or *murrúghach* (from *muir*, sea and *oigh*, a maid), *merrows*, *murdhllcha'n*, *muir-gheilt*, *samhghubha*, and *suir* (sea-nymphs). [84]

Thomas Croker, writing in the book "Fairy Legends and Traditions of the South of Ireland," give us the following description of one of the *maighdean-mhara*:

> "One tremendous blustering day, before he got to the point whence he had a view of the Merrow's rock, the storm came on so furiously that Jack was obliged to take shelter in one of the caves which are so numerous along the coast; and there, to his astonishment, he saw sitting before him a thing with green hair, long green teeth, a red nose, and pig's eyes. It had a fish's tail, legs with scales on them, and short arms like fins: it wore no clothes, but had the cocked hat under its arm, and seemed engaged thinking very seriously about something."[85]

Mermaids were noted in both British and Irish folklore as being both ominous, foretelling disaster, and provoking it. Several variants of the song about St. Patrick tell about a mermaid speaking to doomed ships; in some, she tells them they will never see land again, and in others, she claims they are near shore, which they are wise enough to know means the same thing. They can also be a sign of rough weather.

There is one tale about a woman who was transformed into a mermaid. After 300 years, when Christianity came to Ireland, she appeared before St. Patrick to be baptized, and then she died.

---

[84] Thomas Crofton Croker, *Fairy Legends and Traditions of the South of Ireland*, 243; WB Yeats, *Fairy and Folk Tales of the Irish Peasantry*, 110.

[85] Thomas Crofton Croker, *Fairy Legends and Traditions of the South of Ireland*, 263.

They are known to have to wear a "magical cap," called the *cohuleen druith*, which keeps them safe in their dives below the surface. It is said that if a sea-faerie's magical cap is taken by a human, that person can keep them trapped on land. This is much like the legends of the *selkies* and their seal skins, as we will be talking about in the chapter on Scotland and the *roanes,* talked about later in this chapter.

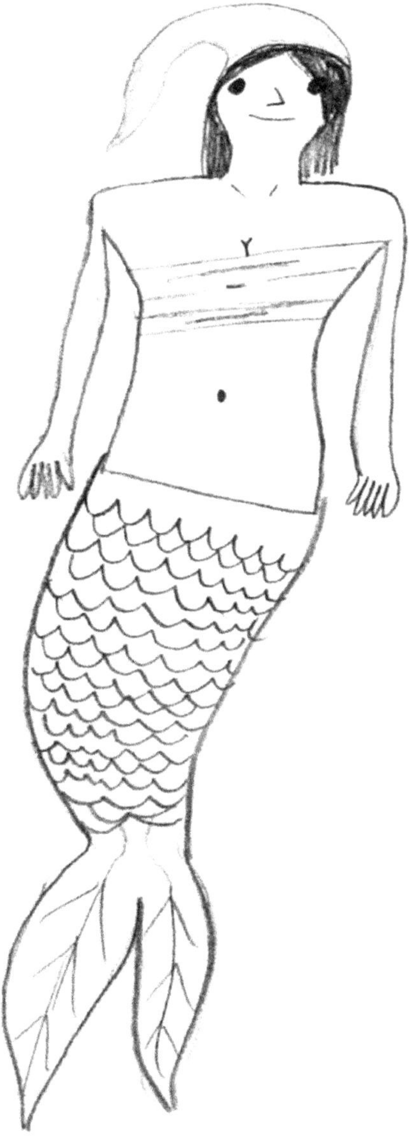

Peists

Next, we have the *peists*. The *peists* are supernatural lake-dwelling creatures, rather like Nessie in Scotland. In both olden times, as told in the tales, and into modern times, they have been seen in some of the lakes in Roscommon, and in a few other lakes. Despite having almost as many people looking for them today as for Nessie, there has been no photographs taken of them.

They are described as being eel-like and very long. Some of the tales put them as large as twenty feet or more. They are said to have a thick body with a large head with a mane like appendage on top of it. According to legend, their main task is to guard treasures that lie on the bottom of the lakes.[86]

[86] Ibid, 432 In the story of the Linn-Na-Payshtha.

Phooka

Moving on, we come to the *phooka*, as it's called in Old Irish. This is another faerie with many regional variations to the name. You may see it as *pooka, púca, puka, phouka, púka*, and *pwwka* in Modern Irish. The *phooka* is a water faerie, and is a great shape-shifter. It may be found in the shape of a dog, horse, bull, goat or even a rabbit in one tale. But, in all instances, its fur is always black or very dark. It most commonly takes the form of a sleek black horse with a flowing mane, and glowing yellow eyes.

If a human is enticed onto a *phooka's* back, it is said that they will get a wild ride. The *phooka* will do the rider no real harm though, unlike the *kelpie*, which we'll talk about when we get to Scotland. The *phooka* has the ability to talk and has been known to give advice, and to lead people away from danger. Though the *phooka* enjoys confusing and often terrifying humans, it is considered benevolent. Samhain Day is the *phooka's* day, and the one-day of the year when it can be expected to behave civilly.[87]

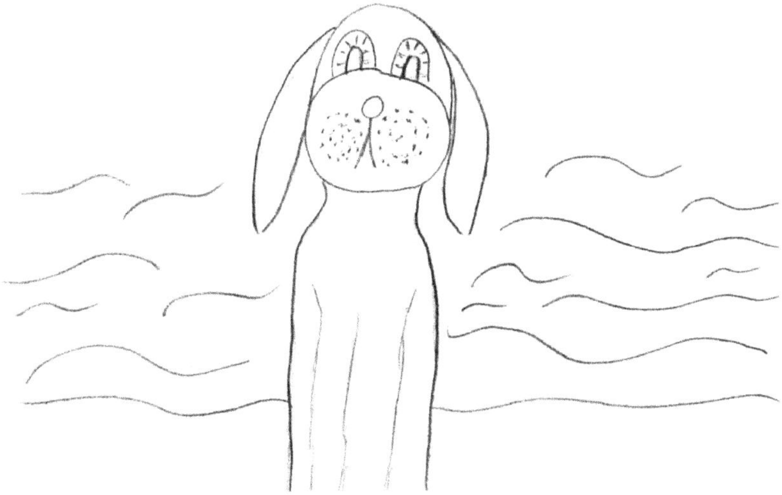

[87] WB Yeats, *Fairy and Folk Tales of the Irish Peasantry*, 152; T. J. Westropp, "A Study of Folklore on the Coasts of Connacht, Ireland (Continued)," 107–171; Larkin, *Faeries*, 109; MacKillop, *Dictionary of Celtic Mythology*, 325 and many others.

Roanes

Next, we have the *roanes*. The *roanes* are the "seal-people" of Ireland, like the "*selkies*" in Scotland. They could shed their skin and live as humans for a while, but they had to return to the sea to restore their health. They are a very gentle folk, and in the tales, one feature that pointed out a woman as a roan, was their big brown eyes.

There are many tales told along the coasts in both Ireland and Scotland about a women who would appear on the beach one day, meet a man and settle down with him, even bearing children to him, but then later disappearing back to the sea. Like the *maighdean-mhara's* magical cap, if their hidden skin wasn't found, then they couldn't go back to the sea until they had it again.

A movie that I feel shows the story of the *roanes* the best is "The Secret of Roan Inish." It was filmed in the Donegal area of Ireland, and it is wonderfully done.[88]

[88] T. J. Westropp, "A Study of Folklore on the Coasts of Connacht, Ireland (Continued)," 118–121; Thomas Crofton Croker, *Fairy Legends and Traditions of the South of Ireland*, 247–249 and many others!.

Sheoques

The *sheoques* are the faeries who live in the thorn bushes, and the ancient stones in the fields of Ireland. It is said that they are the faeries who steal babies and leave "changelings" in their places. Many of the tales talk about the faerie babies and how they wither and die after being left in this world, and many of the tales tell about the methods used to get the human babies back again. We'll be talking more about them in chapter 8.

Differing reasons are given for taking the human babies; some say that the faeries like to keep humans as pets, while others say that the faerie race is dying out and they need new blood to keep it strong. Either way, some of the tales do talk about the human parents going to a nearby place where the faeries show themselves and asking the faeries nicely to give the baby back. In some of the tales, this works!

The usual description for this type of faerie is the small, human looking being, about two feet tall, with wild hair, many times with leaves in it. Many of the tales talk about their usually having a pipe in their mouths or nearby and describe their wonderful dances that take place every night.[89]

[89] Bella Terreno, "Mystical Mythology from around the World" See http://www.bellaterreno.com/art/irish/fairy/irishsheoques.aspx.

Water Sheerie

For our next faerie, we come to the water *sheerie*. Like the English will-o-the-wisps, the water *sheerie* would be seen at twilight, and during the night, on or near the bogs and marshy fields. People would see a light bobbing up and down and think it was another traveler. Many times, they would try to catch up and become hopelessly lost; because whenever they would get close, the water *sheerie* would move away again.

Another name for them is "the jacky lantern," or "corpse candles." This last name comes from what happens to some of the people they trick. Like many of the other solitary faeries, some of the tales show that they are trying to harm, or even kill the humans they lead astray. Some people have been led into patches of quicksand, while others have been led to the edges of cliffs.

While most of the tales only show them as balls of light, some do describe them as dark, goblin-looking creatures. Usually this is what was seen as the last sight of the faerie as they vanished![90]

[90] T. J. Westropp, "A Study in the Legends of the Connacht Coast, Ireland," 111 and others.

Wood Sprites

The wood sprites are tree faeries who favor oak, ash and hawthorn trees. They are similar to the *lunantishee* who inhabit the blackthorn trees and the oakmen of England who inhabit the oak trees. It is said that the only way they would leave their tree was when it was cut down, and then they would follow the human that did it and try to harm, or even kill them if they could.

Many of the Irish peasants thought that these faeries were all that was left of the Druids of old, who had become tree spirits after they were forced out of Ireland, or killed. Others thought that this type of faerie were the remains of an ancient people who had lived in Ireland long before the coming of the Celts. When people started arriving, they "joined" with the trees to keep hidden.[91]

[91] WY Evans-Wentz, *The Fairy-Faith in Celtic Countries*, 64.

By Robert Lee (Skip) Ellison

Manx - *Dinney Mara*

5 ISLE OF MAN[92]

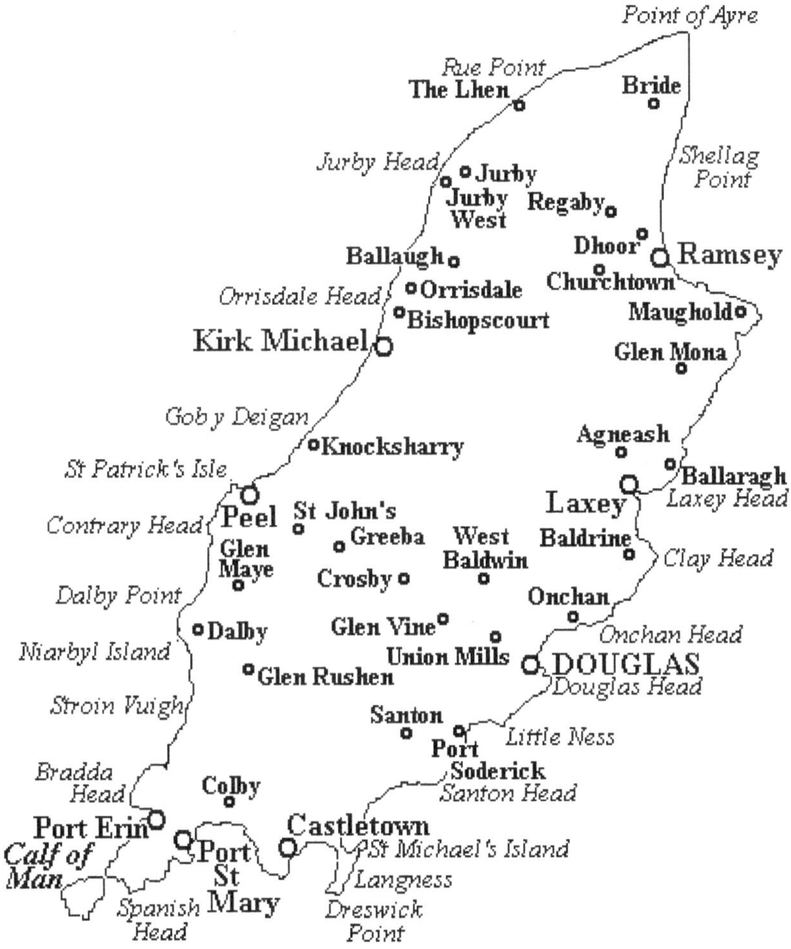

92 "Isle of Man Map."

Adhene

Moving on to the Isle of Man, we start with the *adhene,* which means "themselves" in Manx Gaelic. They were also known as the *cloan ny moyrn,* which means the children of pride. These were the main race of the trooping faeries on the island. Like many of the faerie races, they were easily offended if they were called by the wrong name, so these euphemisms of *adhene* or *cloan ny moyrn* were commonly used.

They could be benevolent, but were mostly mischievous in association with humans. It was said that they were responsible for many of the changelings left on the island. Many people knew to listen for the sounds of building coming from the caves along the sea, for it was said that if the *adhene* were making barrels, the fishing would be good.

They have been described as being child-like in size, and were seen both at sea, while fishing, and in the hills with herds of small faerie cattle.[93]

[93] WILLIAM CASHEN, *MANX FOLK-LORE*, 15.

Buggane

Next, we have the *buggane*, which is the most dangerous and terrifying of all the Manx faeries. This is the evil hobgoblin of the faerie kingdom on the island. *Bugganes* were said to be covered in black hair, and have a large red mouth with tusks. As they were known to tunnel underground, they might be said to resemble a giant mole, though they were intelligent and spoke to people on occasion.

A *buggane* always had a particular home, such as a waterfall, a forest, or an old ruin, where it would remain unless disturbed somehow. The most famous of all is the one associated with the roofless church of St. Trinian's on the main road between Peel and Douglas. This *buggane* repeatedly tore off any new roof that was put back on to the church, terrorizing all around, and to this day the church still has no roof.[94]

[94] See Arthur William Moore, *The Folk-Lore of the Isle of Man: Being an Account of Its Myths, Legends, Superstitions, Customs, & Proverbs, Collected from Many Sources; with a General Introduction; and with Explanatory Notes to Each Chapter*, 60–61 for more details.

Cughtach

Not much is known about our next faerie type. It is called the *cughtach*, or *cughlagh* and is said to be a faerie that haunts caves near the sea. It may be a relative of the *buggane,* or has been conflated with it. While nothing of a harmful nature has been said in any of the tales I have found that talks about it, if it is a relative of the *buggane*, then it likely is harmful.

Their voice is described as sounding like the waves of the sea, but I have been unable to find a description of them. They may be relatives of, or just the Manx version of, the Scottish *cuithac,* which is a type of sea-faerie.[95]

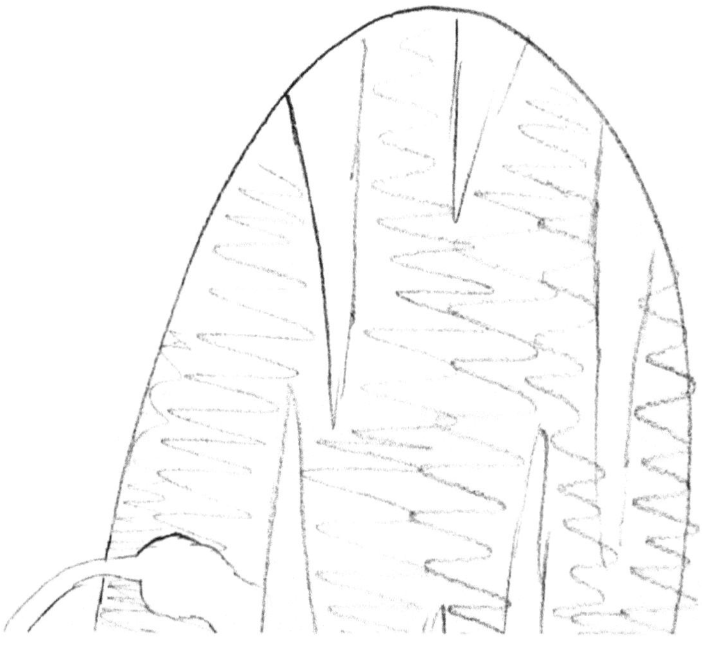

[95] MacKillop, *Dictionary of Celtic Mythology*, 104; Arthur William Moore, *The Folk-Lore of the Isle of Man: Being an Account of Its Myths, Legends, Superstitions, Customs, & Proverbs, Collected from Many Sources; with a General Introduction; and with Explanatory Notes to Each Chapter* and others.

Dinney Mara

Next, we come to the *dinney mara*, or *dooiney marrey*, which is the Manx version of the merman. The name means "Man of the Sea" in Manx. The female version of this faerie, or mermaid, is referred to as *ben-varrey*. He was regarded as friendlier to humans than his counterparts on the coast of England. One piece of folklore about this type of faerie concerns whistling onboard a boat. It was said that whistling would attract the *dinney mara,* and getting his attention would bring bad luck.

It is said that if he were given offerings, then he would help the fishermen bring home big catches. One of the stories told about him tells of a fishing ship manned by seven single men. Each time they went out, they gave offerings of herring to the merman. On each trip, he rewarded them with large catches.

Soon the other fishermen became jealous, and wanted to know how they were doing it. The Harbormaster made them take the other boats with them. During the night, the fishermen who had given him herring heard him say quietly that "It is fine and calm now, but a storm is coming." They hurried back to harbor, but the other boats did not, and they were all lost.[96]

[96] Rose, *Giants, Monsters, and Dragons*, 98.

Dooiney Oie

Our next fairy is the *dooiney oie*, which means night-man in Manx. He is a benign spirit, who warns humans about impending storms. It was said that his howl was loud enough to wake sound sleepers, and if it was heard along the coasts, then the people knew that a great storm would be quickly upon them. Hearing his howl was warning to the farmers to herd their cattle and sheep into a shelter.

The *dooiney oie* is very similar to another Manx fairy, the *howlaa*, which will be talked about later in this chapter. The only difference is that where the *howlaa* howls, the *dooiney oie* speaks.[97]

[97] MacKillop, *Dictionary of Celtic Mythology*, 132 and others.

Ferrishyn

One of the types of trooping faeries in the Isle of Man is known by the name of the *ferrishyn*. This term is plural, and if you are talking about just one of them, the proper term is *ferrish*. The sightings for this type of faeries are prevalent enough that the word *ferrishyn* has become a generic term for all of the faeries in Manx.

In size, they are said to be the same as most of the other trooping faeries in the British isles, about one to three feet in height. One interesting bit of lore that comes down to us talks about how these faeries do not have kings and queens, but consider themselves all equal. While there are a few stories talking about them stealing babies, most of the folktale describe them as being helpful to humans.[98]

[98] Ibid., 192; Arthur William Moore, *The Folk-Lore of the Isle of Man: Being an Account of Its Myths, Legends, Superstitions, Customs, & Proverbs, Collected from Many Sources; with a General Introduction; and with Explanatory Notes to Each Chapter*, 34.

Fireesin

Moving on, we come to the *fireesin*. The *fireesin* is a solitary faerie that helps out around the farms. *Fireesin* means "the harvester" in Manx. Some of the tales talk about why the farmer didn't want their help. This is because they are noted for not being too smart. From the tales, it appears that the *fireesin* did not like the cold, and were not seen during the winter months.

In appearance, they are usually described as being short, nude, with small patches or tuffs of shaggy brown hair on their bodies.[99]

[99] MacKillop, *Dictionary of Celtic Mythology*, 192.

Foawr

Next we come to the *foawr*. They are the giants in Manx tradition. Some folklorists feel that the people of Manx may have based them on the *Formorians* in the Irish Book of Invasions, but these stories come from the countryside, so I am not sure the farmers there would be familiar with the Irish legends.

These giants were not too bad, as giants go. While they would steal cattle to eat, they usually left humans alone, other than throwing large stones if they were bothered. Some of the tales even talk about them flattening barns by throwing boulders on them.[100]

[100] Ibid, 211; John Rhys, *Celtic Folklore - Welsh and Manx*, 285.

Glaisein

Our next faerie is the *glaisein*. The *glaisein* is the grey-haired faerie that lived on farms and helped at night with unfinished chores. It was said that they would help thresh the corn, or find lost sheep and return them to the barns. Many times, they were sighted simply sitting on the hillside watching the farms.

There are modern stories that tell of how the *glaisein* are still around, but since there are not that many farms anymore to help with; they have taken to more activities that are mischievous. It is said that they find large magnetic stones and use them to pull cars off the roads. The *glaisein* is also reported to be a shape-shifter and has been seen as a young grey lamb, or a young grey horse.[101]

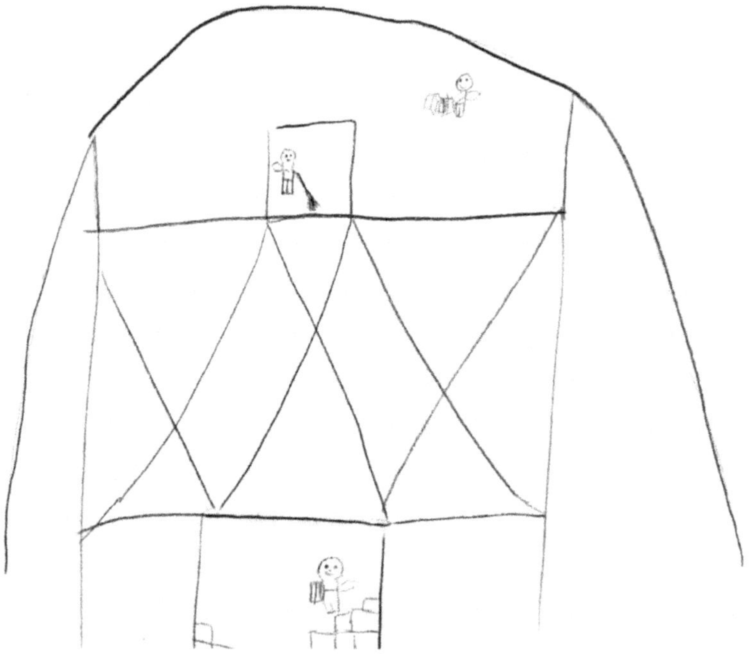

[101] Franklin, Mason, and Field, *The Illustrated Encyclopedia of Fairies*, 106.

Glashtin

Our next fairy is the *glashtin*, which is a Manx water-bull, similar to the *kelpie* in Scotland, or the *phooka* in Ireland. Like many of the water faeries, the *glashtin*, which is also known as the *glashan,* or *glashtyn*, along with tatter-foal, tatter-colt, or shag-foal, is a shape-shifter. It may be seen in the shape of a lamb or small pony or young horse. Where the *kelpie* and *púca* appear as large animals, the *glashtin* is usually depicted as being very small. This is another dangerous faerie, and its favorite pastime according to the tales is catching women alone by the waterside and raping them.[102]

[102] MacKillop, *Dictionary of Celtic Mythology*, 225; "Manx Folk-Lore and Superstitions," 285; Arthur William Moore, *The Folk-Lore of the Isle of Man: Being an Account of Its Myths, Legends, Superstitions, Customs, & Proverbs, Collected from Many Sources; with a General Introduction; and with Explanatory Notes to Each Chapter*, 54, 58–59; John Rhys, *Celtic Folklore - Welsh and Manx*, 285 & 324.

Howlaa

Like the *dooiney oie* talked about above, the *howlaa* is a good faerie who lives along the coasts lines and warns the people of impending storms. The tales about them always speak of their sounds coming from the mountains overlooking the sea. While the *dooiney oie* would talk in their warnings, the *howlaa* was said to issue a howl that sounded like — H-o-w-l-a-a, or H-o-w-a-a.

From the tales, people had learned from experience to listen for the howls of the *howlaa*, and get to shore quickly. It was also said that when the *howlaa* was heard in winter, when the worst storms struck the Isle of Man, that a truly monster storm was on the way and the people would fear so much for their lives that they would stay onshore.[103]

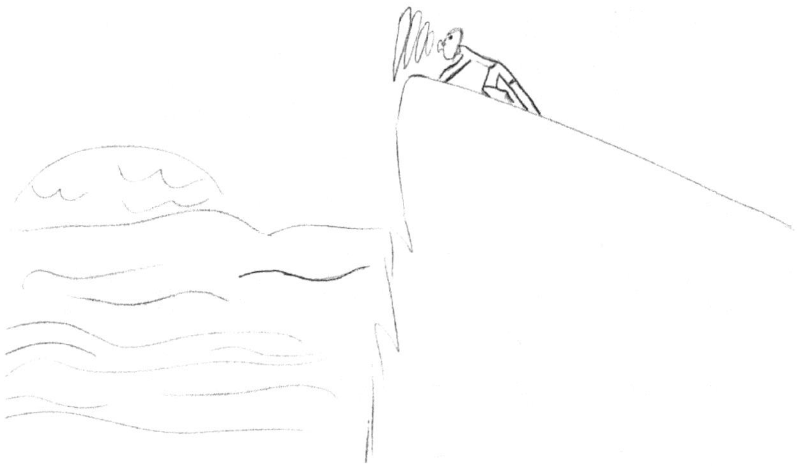

[103] Arthur William Moore, *The Folk-Lore of the Isle of Man: Being an Account of Its Myths, Legends, Superstitions, Customs, & Proverbs, Collected from Many Sources; with a General Introduction; and with Explanatory Notes to Each Chapter*, 50–51.

Lhiannan Shee

Our next fairy, the *lhiannan shee*, is said to be a vampire-like faerie, like the *leanan-sídhe* in Ireland. The tales tell us that when she found a man she wanted, she would "entrance" him to the point where he would do anything for her, but couldn't talk about her with anyone else. It is said that once she had picked a man, she would stay with him until he was drained of all vitality and died. Her name means "faerie sweetheart," and while the man she "bonded with" was happy while he was with her, his life was invariably very short.[104]

Other tales speak of her as a "spirit friend" and as such, she was a guardian of a family. The *lhiannan shee* of Ballfletcher was the family faerie of the Fletchers. It is told that she gave them a "faerie cup," and it was drank from every Christmas in her honor. She is said to haunt wells and springs.[105]

---

104 MacKillop, *Dictionary of Celtic Mythology*, 179–180.

105 Arthur William Moore, *The Folk-Lore of the Isle of Man: Being an Account of Its Myths, Legends, Superstitions, Customs, & Proverbs, Collected from Many Sources; with a General Introduction; and with Explanatory Notes to Each Chapter*, 37.

Moddeh Dhoo of Peel Castle

The next faerie we will talk about is a faerie from one specific location on the Isle of Man, and it is called the *moddeh dhoo* of Peel castle. He is described as being a spectral hound, a large spaniel with curly black hair, and his legend goes back to a time when the castle was a bustling fortress, with its own garrison of soldiers. The black ghostly dog was well known to the soldiers. It was told that he would come into a common room through the walls and lay down near the fire.

Even through it appeared friendly, it was thought that he was capable of terrifying people to death. One of the tales from 1666, tells about a guard, who after drinking a lot, dared the dog to follow him into a small passageway so that he could see if it was a real dog or a devil. After hearing a great noise, the rest of the company found him completely sober and unable to talk. He died three days later and the dog was never seen again.[106]

[106] Ibid, 61–62; WY Evans-Wentz, *The Fairy-Faith in Celtic Countries*, 129; MacKillop, *Dictionary of Celtic Mythology*, 288 & 294.

Phynodderree

Our next faerie from the Isle of Man is the *phynodderree*, which is also seen as *fenodyree* in the Anglicized version. He is another house/farm fairy, like the brownie, who is hard working, but bad tempered. He helps the farmer with chores and is a large, hairy, shaggy elf, usually seen naked. Other tales describe him as appearing as a satyr, with goat like legs. Another name for him is *yn foldyr gastey* (the nimble mower) from his ability to harvest an entire field in one night.[107]

One of the tales recorded in the book "The Fairy-Faith in Celtic Countries," by W.Y. Evans-Wentz tells about a farmer who saw him naked and left out a set of clothes for him. When the faerie found them, he was very unhappy and disgusted that the farmer thought he would "bring himself down enough to wear clothes," and left the farm for good.[108]

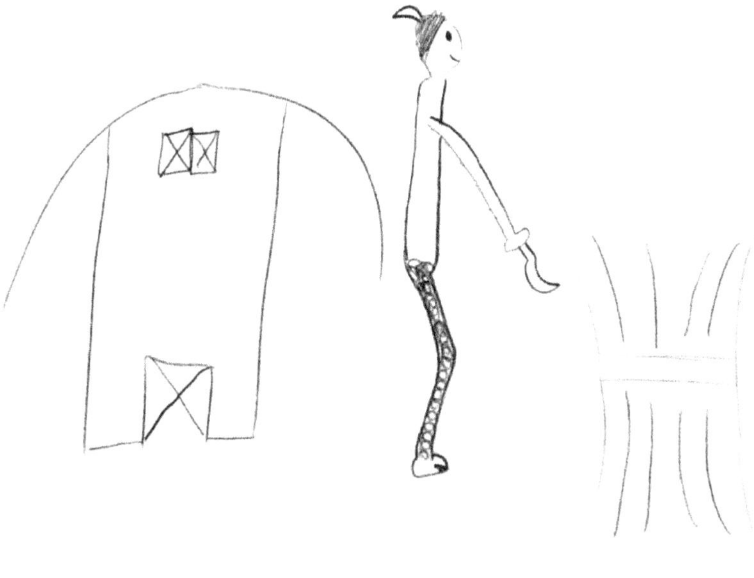

107 MacKillop, *Dictionary of Celtic Mythology*, 187.

108 WY Evans-Wentz, *The Fairy-Faith in Celtic Countries*, 129; John Rhys, *Celtic Folklore - Welsh and Manx*, 286–287; "Manx Folk-Lore and Superstitions," 286.

Tarroo Ushtey (Water Bull)

Our last faerie to talk about from the Isle of Man is the *tarroo ushtey*, or the water bull. This faerie is said to haunt the bogs and wet fields, or live in small ponds. Several of the tales talk about it appearing during the day to mix with the cattle, and when approached by humans, slowly walk back to the pond or bog and disappear. There is even one tale that said he walked away so slowly that the man broke his walking stick over the creatures back and he didn't walk any faster.

A few of the tales do talk about how the *tarroo ushtey* would take cattle back with it to the bogs or ponds and drown them, but these may just be stories made up to explain how the headers lost the cattle. Some of the tales talk about these water bulls mating with the cattle, and unlike the Welsh water bull that gives fertility to the cows, this one only produces monsters. [109]

[109] "Manx Folk-Lore and Superstitions," 284–285; Arthur William Moore, *The Folk-Lore of the Isle of Man: Being an Account of Its Myths, Legends, Superstitions, Customs, & Proverbs, Collected from Many Sources; with a General Introduction; and with Explanatory Notes to Each Chapter*, 59–60; MacKillop, *Dictionary of Celtic Mythology*, 355.

6 SCOTLAND[110]

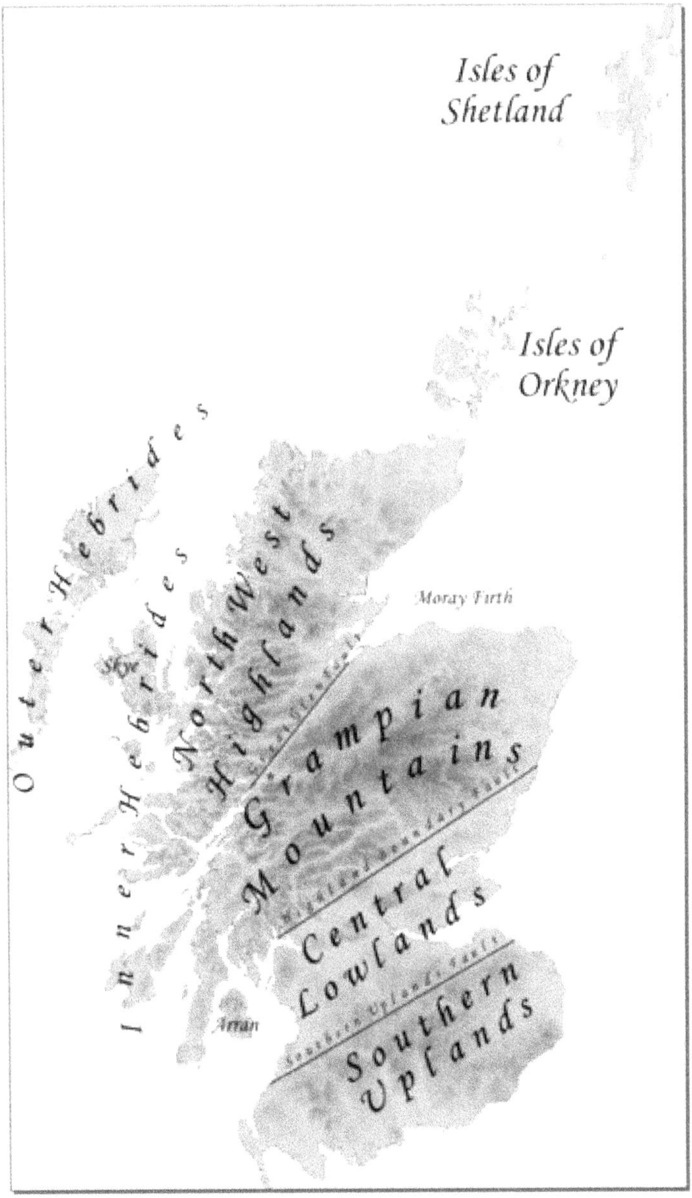

110 "Map of Scotland."

Athach

Our first faerie from Scotland is one that not much is known about. The *athach* is said to be a giant that lives among the cliffs and in lonely lochs in the North of Scotland. While I have not been able to find any folktales about this faerie, the name has come to be synonymous with the English term "giant," so there must have been many tales of it.[111]

[111] MacKillop, *Dictionary of Celtic Mythology*, 25.

Baobhan sìth

Our next fairy, the *baobhan sìth* should not be confused with the *banshee*. In the tales, this faerie is described as being more like the *leanan-sídhe* from Ireland, or the modern tales of vampires. By this, I mean that she sucks the life out of the person she attaches to, and stays with them until they die. All of the tales describe her as very dangerous and as "evil."

Most of the tales about her come from the Highlands, or the Islands of the North. There is a story told about them in the 1909 edition of "The Celtic Review." In it, three men were out hunting and after killing a deer, camped for the night. As two of the men were talking about missing their sweethearts, three women appeared out of the mists, and paired up with the hunters. By morning, two of the men were dead, and only the one that ran from his partner away escaped with his life.[112]

You took our
Prey so now You
are our Prey!

[112] Ms. E. C. Charmichael, *The Celtic Review - Volume 5 - July 1908 to April 1909*, 5:163–165; See also THE GAELIC SOCIETY OF INVERNESS, *Transactions of the Gaelic Society of Inverness Vol XXVI (1904-1907)*, 26:268–269 for more information.

Bean Nighe

Our next faerie, the *bean nighe*, belongs to the class of faeries who are the "washer women at the fords." This type of faerie is prevalent in most of the British Isle countries. The tales tell about people out walking at night seeing her washing bloodstained clothes at a ford in the river or stream, or shore of a lake. Seeing this, they knew that someone in their family or village would soon die.

The tales usually continue to describe her as wearing green, sometimes white, clothes and crying as she works. Unlike the *banshee*, which is usually described as beautiful, the *bean nighe* is almost always described as very ugly, with large buck teeth and long floppy breasts which she has to throw over her shoulders when she works. Regionally in Scotland, the Isle of Islay, and the area around Kintyre have their own versions of this faerie called the *caointeag* (weeper), who is said to be fiercer that those in other areas.[113]

[113] MacKillop, *Dictionary of Celtic Mythology*, 32, 59 & 67; Bella Terreno, "Mystical Mythology from around the World"; Scotl, "Bean-Nighe (Washer Woman)."

Blue Men of the Minch

The blue men are called *na fir horma* in Scots Gaelic, and are water faeries that live in the channel, called the Minch, between the Inner and Outer Hebrides, found on the left side of the map above. They were noted for attacking passing ships in large groups and dragging them under. One of the tales tells us that as long as a captain could keep them talking with riddles or rhymes, they would not attack. If he could keep it up long enough to get out of their territory, then the ship would go free.

They are described as having blue skin with large faces, capped with green hair and usually full green beards. They are also said to have fish-like tails with long arms and are said to be very strong. Their homes are supposed to be in sea caves at the bottom of the channel.[114]

[114] Donald Alexander Mackenzie, *Wonder Tales from Scottish Myth and Legend*, 79–83; "The Blue Men of the Minch"; MacKillop, *Dictionary of Celtic Mythology*, 40.

Bócan

The *bócan*, or *bogan*, is a hobgoblin-like faerie that is a shape-shifter and great trickster. According to the tales, this type of faerie attached itself to the family and would travel great lengths to stay with them. There are even stories of these faeries immigrating with their families to America and Australia.

Although their shape can vary wildly, even from human size to only inches high, some of the tales talk of them being human like, but ugly when they first appear. In several of the tales, they appear to be dangerous to humans, other than the family they attach themselves to, and are not above leading people into situations where they may be killed.[115]

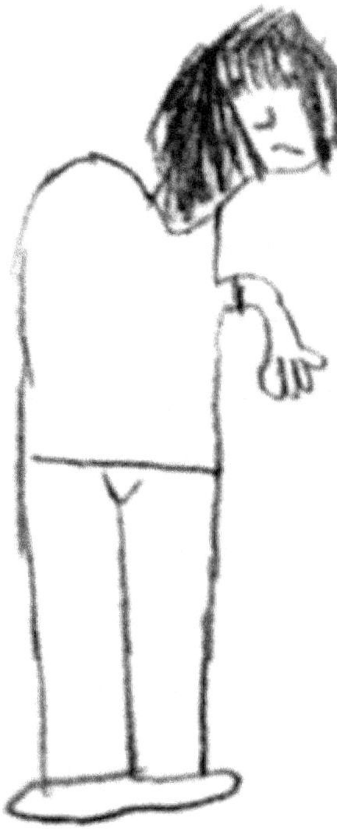

[115] MacKillop, *Dictionary of Celtic Mythology*, 41; W.A. Craigie, "Donald Bán and the Bócan," 353–358.

Boggle

The *boggle* is another type of faerie who is talked about in many tales. The name can also be spelled as *bogle, bogill* or *boggart*. They are familiar to many people today from their inclusion in the Harry Potter films. According to the films, the *boggle* would take the shape of the person's worst fear and could be banished by the *Riddikulus* spell.

Looking to the tales, they were not far off! Many of the tales describe the *boggle* as residing in fields, or wooded areas and jumping out to scare people when they passed by. The *boggles* stayed in the same areas long enough that people would name them, such as the *tatty-boggle* who stayed in the potato fields. Other tales, such as "The Golden Ball,"[116] describe the *boggles* as coming up to cottages at night to scare the folks inside.

One *boggle*, known as Shellycoat, was said to live in the water near docks and play tricks on the fishermen. He would appear as a voice calling out from the sea like a drowning man, luring them far away from the villages. Once they were far away from other people, he would laugh at their foolishness and disappear.[117]

[116] Joseph Jacobs, *More English Fairy Tales*, 13–15.

[117] Mackinlay, James M., *Folklore of Scottish Lochs and Springs*, 168–169; Walter Gregor, *Folk-Lore of the North-East of Scotland*; Sir George Douglas, *Scottish Fairy and Folk Tales*, 181–182 Also see http://en.wikipedia.org/wiki/Bogle for a good list of resources.

Brown Man of the Moors

The brown man of the moors, or *muirs* as some of the tales say, lived in the wild areas of Scotland and didn't want people trespassing on their lands. They were called the brown men due to the color of their clothes, which was said to be brown so that they would blend in with the bracken. They are described as short in statue, about half the size of a man, with wild red hair.

In one of the tales where he is talking to two boys he caught on "his land" he tells them that he is the lord of the area and that all the wild creatures are his subjects. He went on to tell the boys that although he was mortal, he lived far longer than humans and ate only the berries, nuts and apples that grew on the land, and he would not tolerate any animals being killed. The story ends by telling how the brown man tried to get the boys to "cross over a stream" and go with him to his home, but they didn't. One of the boys told the other that if he crossed the running water, he would be torn apart. The one boy that wanted to go with the brown man, fell ill and died within a year of meeting him.[118]

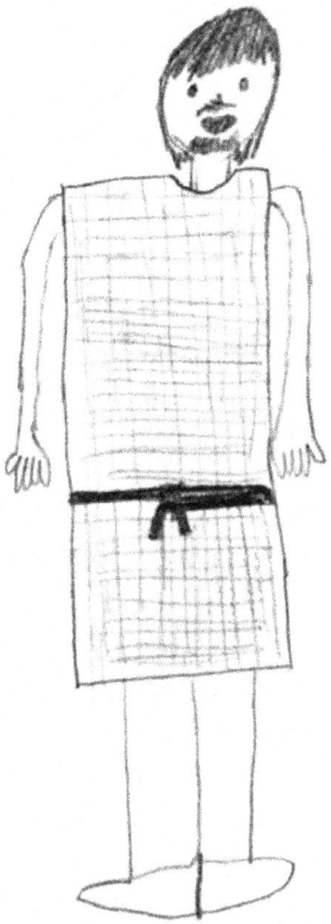

[118] Walter Scott, *The Lady Of The Lake*, 301; Ellen Phillips, *The Enchanted World: Fairies and Elves*, 55–56.

Brownie

Moving on, we come to the Scottish *brownie*. The tales about them are mostly identical with the tales about the English *brownies*, talked about in the chapter on England. They willingly work for a family and do all they can to help them.

One tale tells us about the *brownie's* actions when the mistress of the house unexpectedly started to give birth. The servant who was sent for the midwife wasn't moving with any hurry, so the *brownie* went to get the midwife himself. As they were hurrying back, they had to ford a river that was quickly rising, so the *brownie* picked up the midwife and her horse, and carried them both across. After the midwife was safely taking care of his mistress, the *brownie* give the slow servant a beating for not taking care of his duties.

When the master of the house found out about this, he gave the *brownie* a green coat that the servants had told him the *brownie* admired. Once he laid the coat out, and said that it was for the *brownie*, both the coat and the *brownie* disappeared and were never seen again.[119]

[119] Walter Scott, *Minstrelsy of the Scottish Border, Vol. I (of 3): Consisting Of Historical And Romantic Ballads, Collected In The Southern Counties Of Scotland; With A Few Of Modern Date, Founded Upon Local Tradition.*

Cat Síth - Faerie Cat

Along with the faerie/spectral dogs in the tales, we also have the *cat síth*, which is a faerie cat. It is described as being a black cat with a white spot on its breast, as big as a large dog, with green light shining out of its eyes. While most of the tales talk about this creature as being one of the faeries, others say this this is the spirit of a witch that has been turned into a cat.

In the tale "The King o' the Cats," a man out digging a grave has nine of the cats come up to him with a message. When he gets home and tells his wife about it, his cat sits up and listens intently to the story. At the end of it, when the man tells his wife that he has to tell Tom Tildrum that Tim Tildrum is dead, his cat swells up to giant size and yells, "If Tim Tildrum is dead, then I'm King of the cats!" He then vanished up the chimney like smoke and was never seen again.[120]

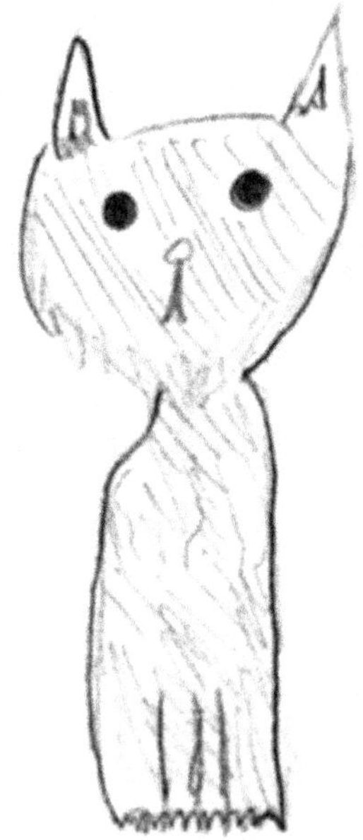

[120] Joseph Jacobs, *More English Fairy Tales*, 169–171.

Ciudach

Our next faerie, the *ciudach*, is very likely a near relative, or even the same faerie under a slightly different name, as the *cughtach* from the Isle of Man. They are a race of faeries who live in caves and deep in the mountains.

There are other tales that describes the *ciudach* as a giant that lives in the mountains. Some of these show them as tolerant of humans, while other later ones say that they prey on humans. Several of the tales center on Mount Schiehallion, which is located ten miles north of Aberfeldy in Perthshire. This mountain has long been regarded as a sacred place where faeries roamed, with tales of long underground caves inhabited by "strange beings."[121]

[121] MacKillop, *Dictionary of Celtic Mythology*, 80.

Crodh Mara

To go along with the faerie dogs and cats, we also have the *crodh mara*, which are the red, or red and white spotted faerie cattle. They are like the *each uisce* of Ireland, but not as dangerous. They are found on or near the west coast of Scotland, in both fresh and salt water.

The stories tell how these faeries would come on land to mate with the cows, or bulls of the local herds. When a female faerie came on shore, she would stay until after her calf was born, if the farmer was fast enough to keep her from getting to the water again. It was said that this improved the entire line of Highland cattle, and some people talk about this still happening today.[122]

122 Ibid, 99–100; The Carmichael Watson Project and Alexander Carmichael, "Story Entitled 'Crodh Marra' [sea-Cattle]"10 entries.

Cù Sìth- Faerie Dog

The *cù sìth* is another faerie dog, like the *moddeh dhoo* of Peel castle in the Isle of Man, or the *youdic* of Brittany. This faerie is described as being the size of a young cow and being green in color, with shaggy fur. Along with being a harbinger of death, this faerie was said to grab up those who were about to die and carry them off to the Otherworld. It was said that they would howl three times when coming for someone. If that person could hide before the third howl, then they would live for a while longer.

Another tales talk about how these faeries were used by the trooping faeries. They were sent out looking for women that were nursing babies, so that they could steal them away to nurse the faerie babies. In times past, dogs howling in the night were always a good reason to stay safely inside![123]

[123] John Gregorson Campbell, *Superstitions of the Highlands and Islands of Scotland*, 30–32.

Dracæ

The *dracæ* are water faeries that try to trap unwary people, usually women, along the shores of their rivers or lakes. They do this by appearing in the shape of gold rings, or gold cups that appear to be just under the water. It is said that when a person reaches under the water to get the cup or ring, then the *dracæ* would grab them and pull them down. They are not supposed to kill the women, just take them to their underground homes to serve as the nurses for their children.

One tale talks about a woman who was captured by these faeries touching her eye with an ointment she found. After that, she always had the ability to see the *dracæ*. This story is a familiar format used for many of the faerie races, and may have been more common in the days of closer interactions between the people and the faeries.[124]

[124] Walter Scott, *Minstrelsy of the Scottish Border, Vol. II (of 3): Consisting Of Historical And Romantic Ballads, Collected In The Southern Counties Of Scotland; With A Few Of Modern Date, Founded Upon Local Tradition*; Sir George Douglas, *Scottish Fairy and Folk Tales*, 124–125.

Fachan

The *fachan* is a one-legged, one-handed, ugly faerie who is said to live in the lonely gorges and wild areas of Scotland. Some of the tales tell us that along with one hand and one leg, the *fachan* also had one eye, one finger, one toe, and only one of all the other body parts a person could see. Another name for them was peg-leg-jack.

This race of faerie was definitely in the group of "not nice" faeries. From the tales, their main goal in life was to drag off and kill unwary travelers. Some of the tales refer to this faerie as a type of *athach*, or giant, that was talked about earlier in this chapter and say that out of all of the faeries the travelers might meet, this was the one feared the most![125]

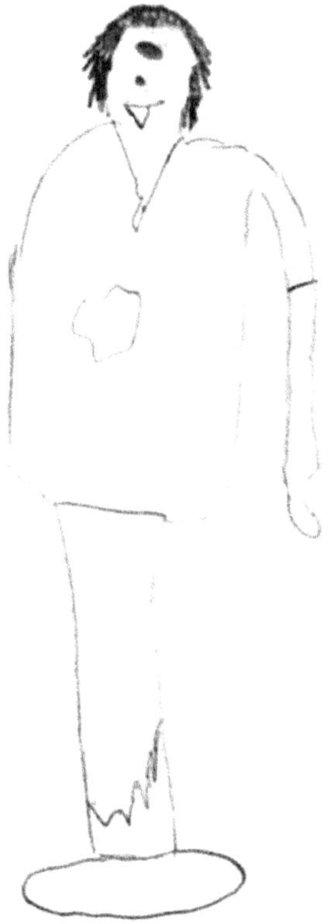

125 Bella Terreno, "Mystical Mythology from around the World"; MacKillop, *Dictionary of Celtic Mythology*, 176; Larkin, *Faeries.*

Fride

Our next faerie is the *fride*, also called *frid, fridich* or *fridean*. They are the faeries who live in, or under rocks and eat up the crumbs of spilled food that people drop. They are also said to guard the roads, and travelers would leave out crumbs of food, or spill some milk for them before they left on a trip.

If the crumbs were left for them, they would guard a person's property, and their animals as well. In the journal "The Celtic Review," we hear the following in a longer story:

> "Macmhuirich Mor went home, and though he never went into his kitchen before, he went in that day. His baking woman was making bread, and bits of dough and grains of meal were falling from her in the process. She took no notice of these till a piece fell from the bannock on her palm, and then she stooped down and lifted it. Macmhuirich noticed her, and he went over and gave her a tap on the back of the hand with the switch he had, saying, '*Gabh ealla ris, a mhuirneag, is ioma bial feumach tha feitheamh air* * – * Leave it alone, maiden, many a needful mouth is waiting for it. And as long as thou shalt stand in my house never again remove the fragments of food from the floor, they are the rightful dues of '*fridich nan creag*,' the gnomes of the rocks.' "[126]

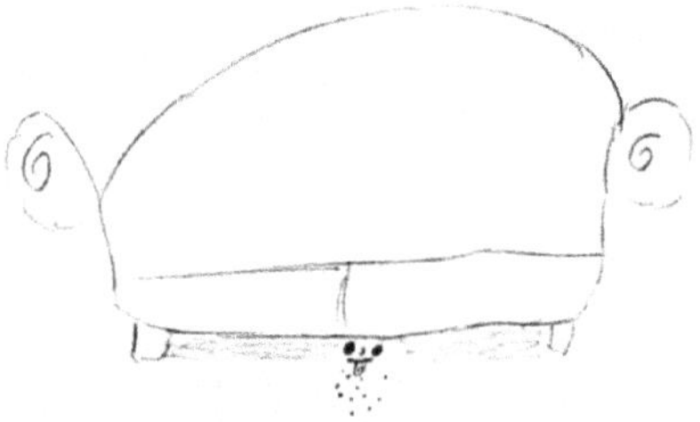

[126] Ms. E. C. Charmichael, *The Celtic Review - Volume 5 - July 1908 to April 1909*, 5:69–70.

Ghillie Dhu

Next, we move on to the g*hillie dhu,* which means dark boy in Scots Gaelic. These are Scottish faeries that dress in foliage, and act as tree guardians. In the tales, they dislike humans and jealously guard their trees from them. These faeries once heavily populated Scotland but are rarely seen anymore. *Ghillie dhu* are said to be about seven inches tall with light green skin and wild black hair. They are described as being thin, with long arms and fingers. They wear clothing made from knitted grass and mosses with leaves stuck in to help camouflage them. Another illustration of them can be found on page 10 above.

The g*hillie dhu* are very shy, docile creatures that protect the woods around them from destruction by man or natural storms. They are said to live in nests in the tree branches, almost like squirrel nests, or in hollows in the trees. In modern times, their first name, *ghillie*, has been adopted to name a type of suit worn by snipers and hunters to blend in with the terrain.[127]

[127] MacKillop, *Dictionary of Celtic Mythology*, 223; Bella Terreno, "Mystical Mythology from around the World."

Glaistig

Our next faerie, the *glaistig*, which means water imp, is a faerie that haunts lonely places around lakes and rivers. She, they are almost always female, is usually said to be a beautiful woman on the top half, but with the bottom half of a goat. Like many of the faerie types, she is said to dress in green, with a long flowing dress that covers her bottom half. Her skin is described as greyish, and she usually has long blond hair, down to her feet in some of the tales.[128]

Many of the tales describe her as a "demon lover," like the *baobhan sìth* talked about earlier in this chapter. In these tales, she lures young men to wild areas and then kills them and drains their blood.

In other tales, she is described as the protector of the cattle herds. In these tales, offerings of milk were given to her for her aid in keeping the cattle safe.[129] The faerie we'll talk about in a few pages, the *gruagach*, is often described this same way, and I believe the two may have simply been mixed up, and the demon lover is the correct description of her.

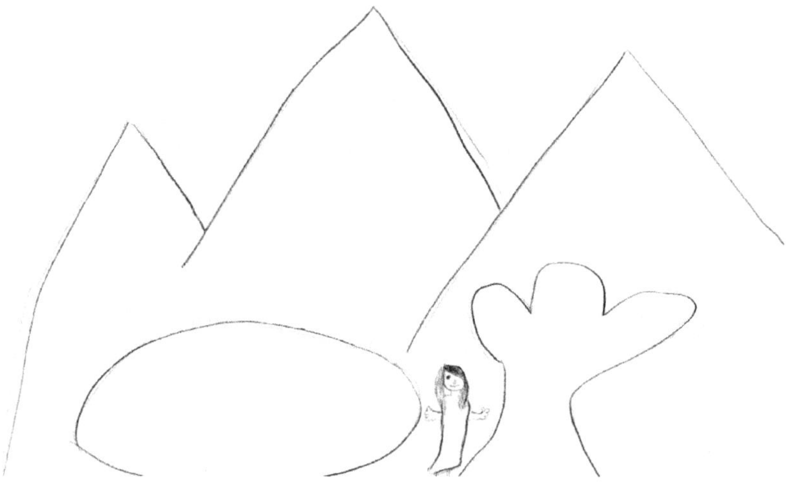

[128] Richard Mercer Dorson, *History of British Folklore, Volume 1*, 417.
[129] "Glaistig."

Green Woman

We find our next faerie located near the Moray Firth, in the upper northeast section of Scotland. She is called the Green Woman, and it is said that she would visit cottages at night to steal children. Modern folklorists believe that her legend was created to explain Sudden Infant Death syndrome, at a time when there was no scientific explanation. Her tales tell us that she always wore green, and didn't bother anyone else, except the babies and their parents.

She was described as wearing green, and many times was seen carrying a "sickly, wrinkled demon child with fiery eyes and sharp-pointed little fingers."[130] When she found a cabin with a baby in it, she would wait until everyone was asleep then creep in. It was said that she would then kill the human child and use its blood to bathe her baby to make it healthy again.

[130] Time-Life Books, *The Enchanted World: Night Creatures*, 43.

Gruagach

In some of the tales, the *gruagach* was known as the queen of the faeries who guarded the cattle. In "The Fairy-Faith in Celtic Countries," W.Y. Evans-Wentz tells us:

> "The fairy queen who watches over cows is called *Gruagach* in the Islands, and she is often seen. In pouring libations to her and her faeries, various kinds of stones, usually with hollows in them, are used… In many parts of the Highlands, where the same deity is known, the stone into which women poured the libation of milk is called *Leac na Gruagaich*, 'Flag-stone of the *Gruagach*.' If the libation was omitted in the evening, the best cow in the fold would be found dead in the morning."[131]

Other references describe the *gruagach* as an old God who had turned into a *brownie*. In these tales, the faerie is usually described as a handsome man.[132]

[131] WY Evans-Wentz, *The Fairy-Faith in Celtic Countries*, 92–93.

[132] "The Religion of the Ancient Celts: Chapter XVI. Sacrifice, Prayer, and Divination," 246; MacKillop, *Dictionary of Celtic Mythology*, 230.

Gyre Carlin

For our next faerie, we move to the Fife area of Scotland, which is located in the Middle Eastern section of the country. The queen of the faeries in this area was known as the *Gyre Carlin.* This is also seen as *Gyre-Carlin*, *Gy-Carling*, or *Gay-Carlin*. These variations all relate in some way to greedy old women or witch. In some of the tales, she is called *Nicneven*, *Nicnevin* or *Nicnevan*. These variations refer to daughter of a saint or daughter of the divine, or "bone-mother." While some of the tales say she was very beautiful, and interacted well with the humans in the area, most describe her as a witch, or the mother of witches, who flew through the air.

A few of the tales associate her with spinning, and if there was unfinished spinning left at the new year, the *Gyre Carlin* would take it.[133]

133 "Nicnevin or Gyre Carlin"; David Laing LL.D, *Select Remains of the Ancient Popular and Romance Poetry of Scotland*, 271–275.

Headless Trunk

Our next faerie is found on the Isle of Skye, the largest and most northerly island in the Inner Hebrides, which is on the Northwest side of Scotland. It is called the headless trunk and is reported to be a large, headless monster, who murders only men, never women or children. Unlike some of the other headless faeries we have discussed, there is no mention of this one carrying its head with it.

John Campbell, writing in "Popular Tales of the West Highlands" was told a tale about the headless trunk, which he called the *coluinn gun cheann,* by a dancing master. He felt that the faerie being described in the tale was actually a *bócan.* He said that the faerie was always associated with the Macdonald's of Morar, and could be seen near Morar House. He was always looking for strong men to test his strength against.[134]

[134] John Francis Campbell, *Popular Tales of the West Highlands*, 101–103; Mirino, "Viewfinder."

Kelpie

Next, we talk about the *kelpie*. The *kelpie* is a Scottish water faerie. It is usually seen in the shape of a beautiful horse standing near a creek or river. Sometimes, it will only give the person that mounts on it a dunking the creek, but will not harm them further. However, other times, the *kelpie* was said to lure humans, especially children into the water to kill and eat them. It usually does this by encouraging children to ride on its back, where its skin becomes adhesive, and it then drags them to the bottom of the water and devours them - except for the heart or liver.[135]

A common Scottish tale is the story of nine children lured onto a *kelpie*'s back, while a tenth child keeps his distance. The *kelpie* chases him and tries to catch him, but he escapes. A variation on this is that the tenth child simply strokes the *kelpie's* nose, but when his finger becomes stuck to it, he takes out a knife from his pocket, and cuts his own finger off. He saves himself, but is unable to help his friends as they are pulled underwater with the *kelpie*.[136]

135 Keightley, Thomas, *The Fairy Mythology*, 360,385; Mackinlay, James M., *Folklore of Scottish Lochs and Springs*, 162–165.

136 "Kelpie."

Lorreag

We stay in the Hebrides for our next faerie, the *lorreag*. She is a faerie who acts as a patron of spinners. It is said that she appears as an old woman, wearing white, and is an expert at spinning, more than willing to punish whoever is lax or careless at it. It is said that if someone is not spinning according to tradition, she will make their work vanish so they have to start over correctly. A garment woven by her was said to keep ailments from the wearer.

It is said that above all other gifts from human spinners, she liked milk and cream from the cows. In size, they are small, and some of the tales describe then a child-like, or even the size of newborn children. She also loves music and will tease or taunt anyone singing off key.[137]

137 "Loireag."

Nuckelavee

Our next type of fairy is the *nuckelavee*, also seen as *nucklelavee* or *nuchlavis*. This is another type of faerie that is not very nice. The *nucklelavees* are one type of Scottish sea faeries. We find a good description of this type of faerie in the book "Scottish Fairy and Folk Tales," by Sir George Douglas. He tells us in one of the tales about the fairy:

> "...He soon discovered to his horror that the gruesome creature approaching him was no other than the dreaded *Nuckelavee*. The lower part of this terrible monster, as seen by Tammie, was like a great horse with flappers like fins about his legs, with a mouth as wide as a whale's, from whence came breath like steam from a brewing-kettle. He had but one eye, and that as red as fire. On him sat, or rather seemed to grow from his back, a huge man with no legs, and arms that reached nearly to the ground. His head was as big as a clue of simmons (a clue of straw ropes, generally about three feet in diameter), and this huge head kept rolling from one shoulder to the other as if it meant to tumble off. But what to Tammie appeared most horrible of all, was that the monster was skinless; this utter want of skin adding much to the terrific appearance of the creature's naked body,--the whole surface of it showing only red raw flesh, in which Tammie saw blood, black as tar, running through yellow veins, and great white sinews, thick as horse tethers, twisting, stretching, and contracting as the monster moved..."[138]

[138] Sir George Douglas, *Scottish Fairy and Folk Tales*, 198–200; Larkin, *Faeries.*

It was also said that the *nuckelavee* had an odor like rotten fish or eggs, and that his breath alone was enough to wilt plants, or to cause strong people to faint. According to the tales, the only way to escape from a *nuckelavee* was to cross running **fresh** water, which the *nuckelavee* could not do. One of the tales talks about a *nuckelavee* being splashed by fresh water as it was chasing a person, and the *nuckelavee* reacted as if it was splashed by acid.

Peg Powler

Another river hag was Peg Powler, who was found in the River Tees in the North of England/South of Scotland areas. Many of the reports tell of her green or blue skin, like that of one long dead. It was said that like Jenny Greenteeth, found further south in England, she would catch the ankles of those who wandered too close to the river and pull them in to their death.

It was also said that river fish would clean the scraps of meat stuck in her teeth from the children she ate, and so keep her teeth sharp. This type of water fairy, including Jenny Greenteeth, are prevalent enough in the British isles, that they are classified as *grindylows*, which probably comes from the Anglo-Saxon name Grendal.[139]

[139] John Harland and T. T. Wilkinson, *Lancashire Folk-Lore: Illustrative of the Superstitious Beliefs and Practices, Local Customs and Usages of the People of the County Palatine*, 53; "Grindylow"; "Peg Powler."

Selkies

Our next faerie, the *selkie* is found all around the coasts of Scotland. Like the Irish *roanes,* they are sea faeries that can change into human form from seals. There are many tales that have come down to us about a fishermen who would see a seal come ashore, and then make the change into a beautiful woman. He would fall in love with her, or her with him, and they would live together until it was the *selkie's* time to go back into the sea. This might be because she had found her skin, if it was being hidden by the fisherman, or if she grew homesick, if her skin wasn't being hid.

On the Shetland Islands, these faeries were referred to a sea-*trows*. We'll be talking about *trows* later and they are very different, so this might have just been used as a generic term for faerie in this instance. It was said to be very bad luck to injure a *selkie,* and one of the tales talks about how when one was shot, a great storm arose as soon as the *selkie's* blood touched the sea.[140]

[140] Time-Life Books, *The Enchanter World: Water Spirits*, 108–115; Mackinlay, James M., *Folklore of Scottish Lochs and Springs*, 4–5.

Shoney

Our next faerie may be either a faerie who helps bring in the seaweed, or one of the old Gods or Goddesses. He, or she for both are used in the tales, is Shoney and the stories about him or her come from the island of Lewis, among the Western Islands. The name may also be seen as Shony, Shoni or Soni.

The tales tell us that each year on Hallowtide, a corruption of All Hallows Eve, or what is more commonly known as Samhain or Halloween - October 31, the people of the villages along the shores would gather in the churches and prepare libations for Shoney in exchange for a bountiful harvest of seaweed. These libations were special grains that had been gathered throughout the growing season, then brewed into malt liquor or ale.

It was told how the people would carry out large pitchers of ale and pour it into the sea while saying, "Soni, Soni! send us plenty of seaware this year and we will give thee more ale next year."[141] After the offerings were given, the people would return to the churches and blow out a special candle that had been burning to Shoney on the altar, then go out into the fields to spend the remainder of the night in dancing and singing.[142]

141 John Abercromby, "Traditions, Customs, and Superstitions of the Lewis," 165.
142 WY Evans-Wentz, *The Fairy-Faith in Celtic Countries*, 93.

Sìthiche

Our next faerie, the *sìthich,* or *sìthiche* is a bothersome faerie who loves to torment pregnant women. In the Scottish Highland tales, this is the usual type of faerie that steals newborn babies. In many areas of Scotland, this name has come to mean simply elf, or faerie. In many of this tales, this term is used to denote any of the household faeries. The term *sìthiche* is singular, and when you are referring to more than one of this type of faerie, the proper term is *sìthichean.*[143]

In the early 17th century, this type of faerie was denounced by churchmen for shooting "elf stones" at people and hurting them. This is interesting considering that another meaning of the word *sìthich* is "peace" or "calm."[144]

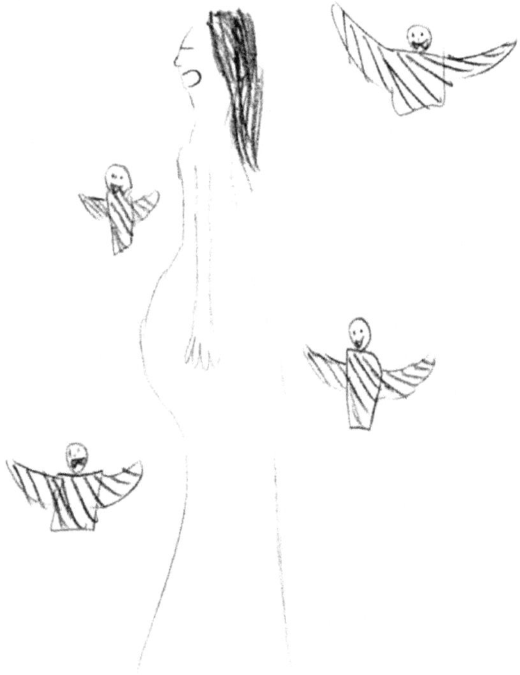

[143] en.wiktionary.org, "Sìthiche - Scots Gaelic."

[144] George Henderson, *Survivals in Belief Among the Celts*, 253; MacKillop, *Dictionary of Celtic Mythology*, 342.

Sluag

Our next race of faerie is found in the Highlands of Scotland and is the *sluag*. This may also be seen as *sluagh* or *sluagh-síthe*. The *sluag* are known as the host of the Unforgiven, or Restless Dead, and is another faerie race that does not deal well with humans. There is some speculation that this might be a very old race of faeries, and that it was known to the original Pictish people of Scotland.

Sometimes they were thought of as generally evil people, who were not welcome in heaven, hell, or in the Pagan Otherworld. It is said that these faeries had also been rejected by the Pagan deities, and by the Earth itself. Whatever the underlying belief, either Christian or earlier Pagan, they are almost always depicted as troublesome and destructive.

They were said to fly in groups like flocks of birds, coming from the west, and were known to try to enter the house of a dying person in Christian times, in an effort to carry the soul away with them. West-facing windows were sometimes kept closed to keep them away. Some say the *sluag* would also carry with them the souls of innocent people, who were kidnapped by these destructive spirits.[145]

[145] MacKillop, *Dictionary of Celtic Mythology*, 343 and others.

Trows

For our next faerie, the *trows*, we move back to the Northern Islands. The *trows*, also called *drows*, are found mainly in the legends of the Orkney and Shetland islands. They are said to be very much like the trolls of Scandinavia - short, ugly, nocturnal, and shy.

They are said to inhabit the caves along the shores and in some of the tales are conflated with the *selkies*, which are called sea-*trows*. It is likely that these faeries came to the islands with the Norse who invaded these islands early in their history. *Trows* are said to be fond of music and that they will creep out of their caves in the night to listen to it.

Many of the *trows* inhabited the same area long enough that they were named by the people. Two names that have come down to us are Truncherface (trencher face) and Bannafeet (bannock feet).[146]

[146] Sigurd Towrie, "The Trows."

Urisk

The name of our next faerie, the *urisk*, is the Lowland Scots name for a type of *brownie*. According to some of the tales, this faerie is a solitary faerie that lives near pools of water. It is said that they are extremely lonely, and try to find friendship among humans, but because of their horrifying appearance, people run from them.[147]

Other tales describe them as a very friendly type of house faerie, very much like the English *brownie*. They talk about the families leaving bowls of cream out for them, and the faeries leaving the household if they were not treated well. [148]Perhaps both kinds lived in the area, and the solitary ones were just faeries that had been mistreated?

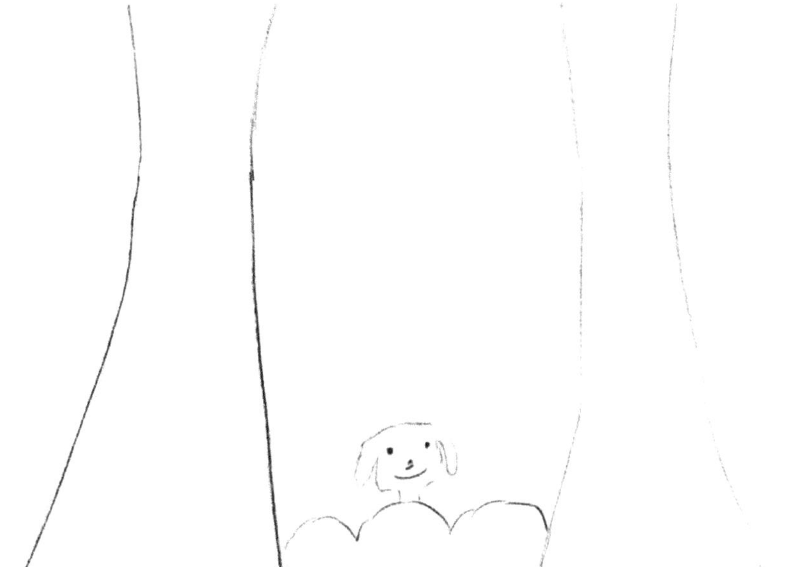

147 Keightley, Thomas, *The Fairy Mythology*, 396.
148 Electric Scotland, "Social History of the Highlands: Superstitions."

Wilkie

We go back to the Orkney Islands for our last fairy from Scotland, the *wilkie*. Little is known about this faerie, other than what we have from a letter written in 1833 by a Mr. J. Paterson. In it, he said:

> "Of two burial mounds (in one of which an urn was found) near Pier-o-wall, Westray, known as Wilkie's Knolls'] the Orcadians can give no information who this Wilkie was. But there is a tradition prevalent that all the natives of Westray were in the habit of dedicating to him daily a certain proportion of milk. This milk was poured into a hole in the centre of one of the tumuli. It is also said that if any either refused or neglected to give him this portion of milk, that their clothes or other articles which might be exposed, would be stolen ; that they, and their cattle, would be in danger of being inflicted with disease, while their houses would be haunted by him… It is still customary for the natives to frighten their children to silence by telling them that 'Wilkie's coming."[149]

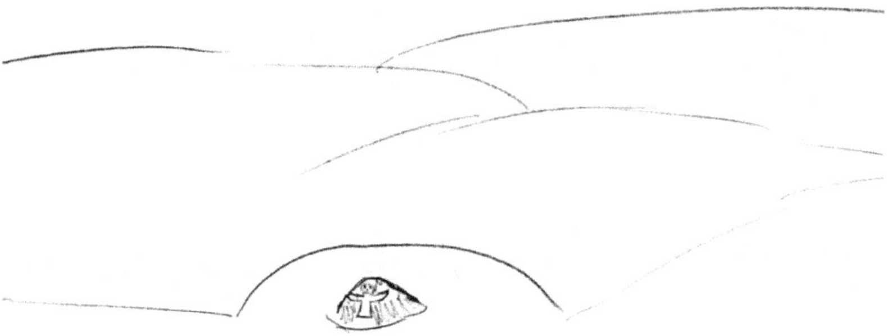

[149] George Fraser Black and Northcote Whitridge Thomas, *Examples of Printed Folk-Lore Concerning the Orkney & Shetland Islands, Volume 3*, 47.

7 WALES[150]

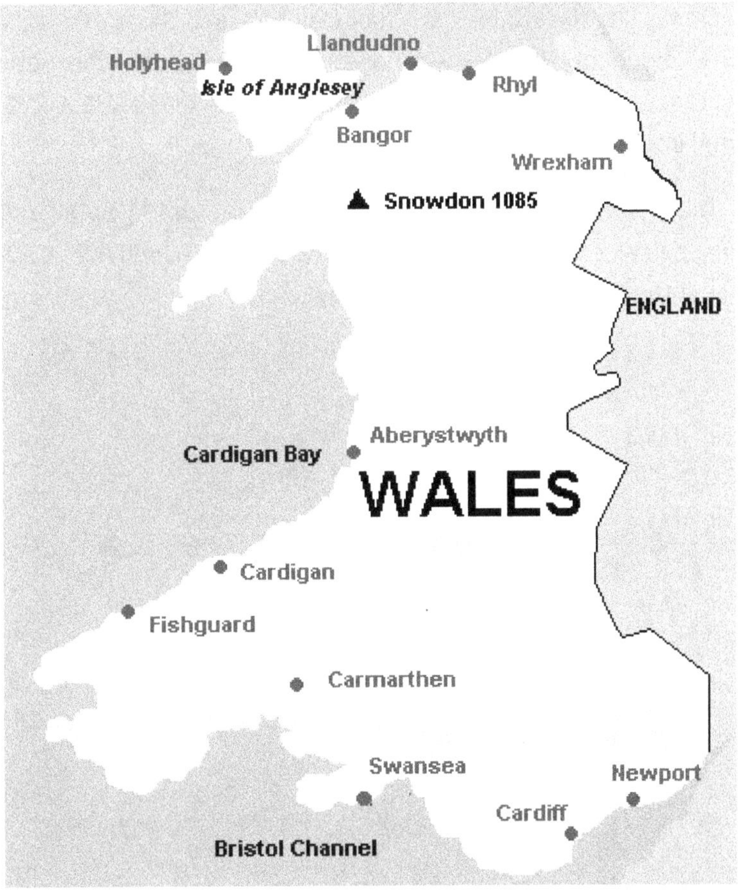

150 "Map of Wales."

Afang

We start our tour of the Welsh faeries with the *afang*. The *afang* was described as a terrible monster, a dragon really from the description, which lived on the bottom of a large bog. He is said to have a long tail that could wrap itself around a mountain. Along its back, was a ridge of horns, like spines, and higher than an alligator's.

On his head, were big ears, half way between those of a jackass and an elephant. His eyes were as green as leeks, and were round, but scalloped on the edges, like squashes, while they were as big as pumpkins.

There is a great tale told of how he was captured by a beautiful young girl, whose perfume caused him to fall in love with her. And as most of these tales, this lead to his downfall.[151]

[151] William Elliot Griffis, *Welsh Fairy Tales - Griffis - 1921*, 5–15.

Bendith y Mamau

Moving on, we come to the *bendith y mamau*, which means "The Mothers' Blessing" in Welsh. Some people say that this is simply a euphemism for all of the Welsh faeries, but others say that they are a specific race within the faeries. The main description of them says that they are short and ugly, with long, misshapen withered limbs. It is also said that they have long, unkempt hair that hangs in bunches and only covers part of their heads. It is thought that they are the result of crossbreeding between goblins and faeries. They are usually bad tempered and want to be left alone.

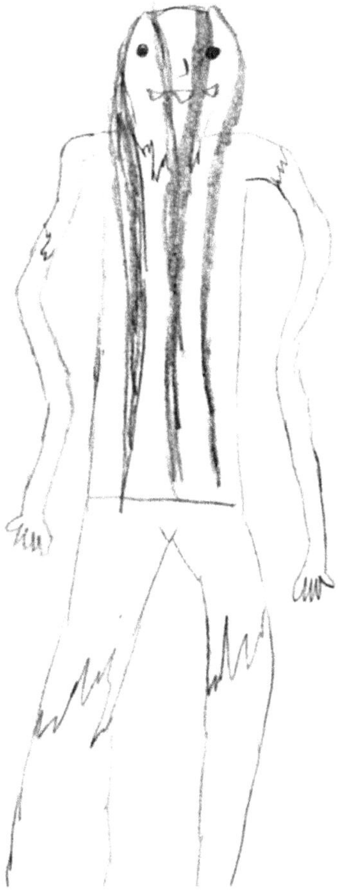

Their children are called *crimbils*, and are said to be exceedingly ugly. The *bendith y mamau* tries to steal human babies, while leaving their own child in the humans place. There are ways described to get your child back if it has been taken, but they are involved and many times harsh on the supposed changeling. It is said that a returned child will remember nothing of its time with the *bendith y mamau*, except for a vague recollection of sweet music. The *bendith y mamau* while not pleasant to be around, are not abusive to the children, in fact they are treated fairly well according to the tales.[152]

[152] MacKillop, *Dictionary of Celtic Mythology*, 36; Thomas Powell, *Y Cymmrodor: The Magazine of the Honourable Society of Cymmrodorion*, 125–141.

Bwca

Our next faerie is the Welsh version of the house faerie, and is called the *bwca*. You may also see this as *bwbach* or *boobach*. They are noted for helping the household churn the butter, but only if the fireplace is kept clean, and if there is a bowl of cream left out for them each night. If the *bwca* is not happy with the family, then it will throw things, bang about and make noise at night, and tell the family secrets to the other people in the village. When they turn nasty, they are **very** hard to get rid of.

One of the tales tells about a time when a maid, trying to hurt the family she worked for, left out a bowl of urine for the *bwca* instead of cream. Needless to say, the *bwca* was not happy, and after causing a great deal of hardship for the family, left and moved into a neighboring farm.[153]

[153] MacKillop, *Dictionary of Celtic Mythology*, 58; Wirt Sikes, *British Goblins: Welsh Folk-Lore, Fairy Mythology, Legends and Traditions*, 30–33, 133, & 157.

Bwciod

Moving on, we come to the *bwciod*. He is a solitary faerie who is said to be small, about one foot high, with purple eyes and a long pointed nose. It is said that he moves very fast, too fast even to see. He loves to warm himself at the hearth, but he will turn nasty if people try to keep him away from the fire.[154]

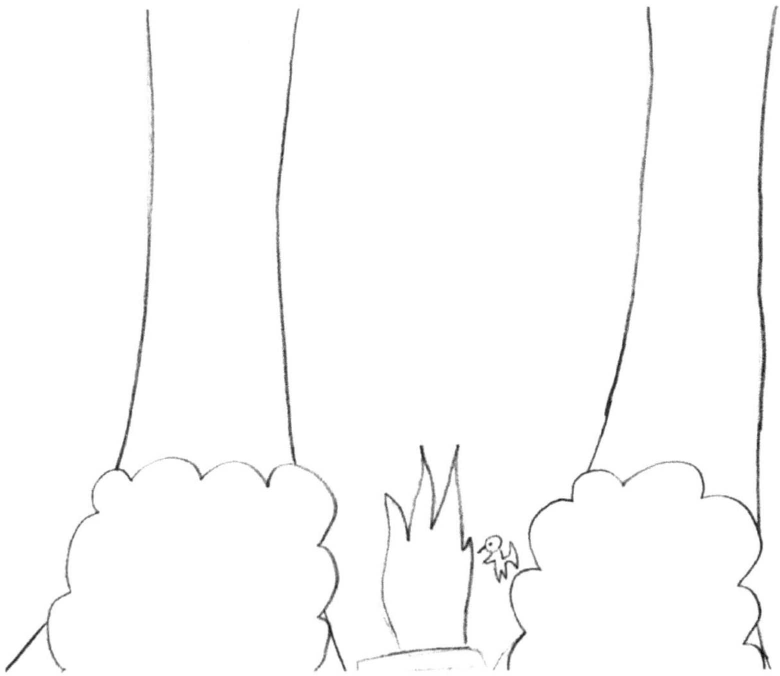

[154] Franklin, Mason, and Field, *The Illustrated Encyclopedia of Fairies*, 40.

Bwgan

Our next faerie is the *bwgan*, if you are referring to one fairy, or the *bwganod*, if you are referring to more than one. These are the Welsh goblins. It is said that they would live in the countryside and frighten travelers if they were out late at night. People would report hearing the noise of working coming from the bottom of ponds, or the voices of children crying out from the depths of those ponds, but upon investigation, nothing would be found.

It was said that they appeared soon after dark, and were active all through the night. Along with being a goblin used to scare children, as in "the *bwganod* will get you if you stay out after dark," many adults would admit they were scared of them as well.[155]

[155] WY Evans-Wentz, *The Fairy-Faith in Celtic Countries*, 45; MacKillop, *Dictionary of Celtic Mythology*, 58; John Rhys, *Celtic Folklore - Welsh and Manx*, 67–68.

Ceffyl y Dwfr: The Water Horse

The *ceffyl y dwfr* is the Welsh version of the Irish *phooka* or the Scottish *kelpie*. Like them, he is said to dwell in bodies of water, in this case either fresh or salt water. Also like them, he wants to find people who are willing to get on his back, and when they do, he will take them into the water and drown them.

The tales tell how the only people who could ride the *ceffyl y dwfr* were clergymen, or people who rode with them. It was said that if you wanted to call up a *ceffyl y dwfr*, you could shake a bridle over a body of water where one lived and he would appear on the shore.[156]

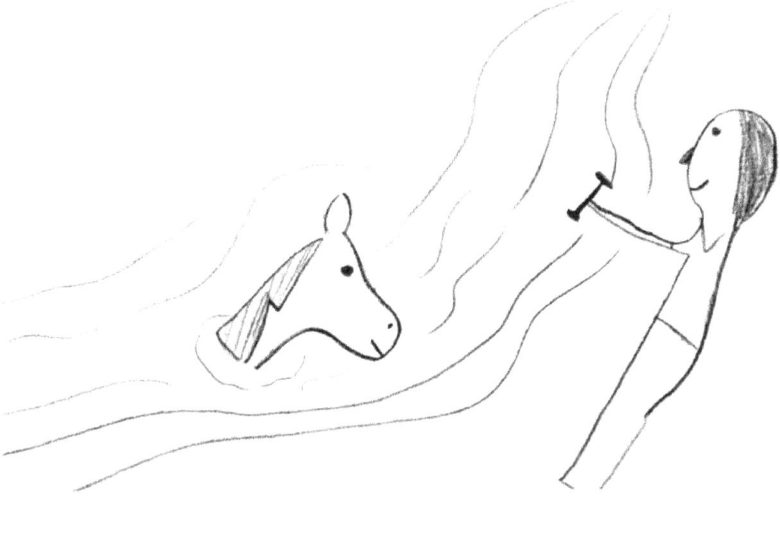

[156] REV. ELIAS OWEN, *Welsh Folk-Lore - Owen - 1887*, 97–99; MacKillop, *Dictionary of Celtic Mythology*, 58.

Coblynau

Moving on, we come to the *coblynau*, who are the Welsh mine spirits. They are similar to the Cornish *knockers*, or the German *kobolds*. These mine spirits were "good faeries," and helped the miners by knocking in places with rich veins of minerals. It is said that the *coblynau* dressed in miners' attire, were ugly to look at, and stood at around 18 inches in height. It is also told that they were very good-natured, and would help the miners in any way they could, as long as the miners didn't make fun of them. If the miners were not nice, then they would turn nasty, and throw rocks at the miners.

Working all day in the dark, closed-in space of a mine, it is easy to see how the belief in these faeries came about. There are many noises underground, and to the miners, it was obvious that the noises **must** come from the faeries![157]

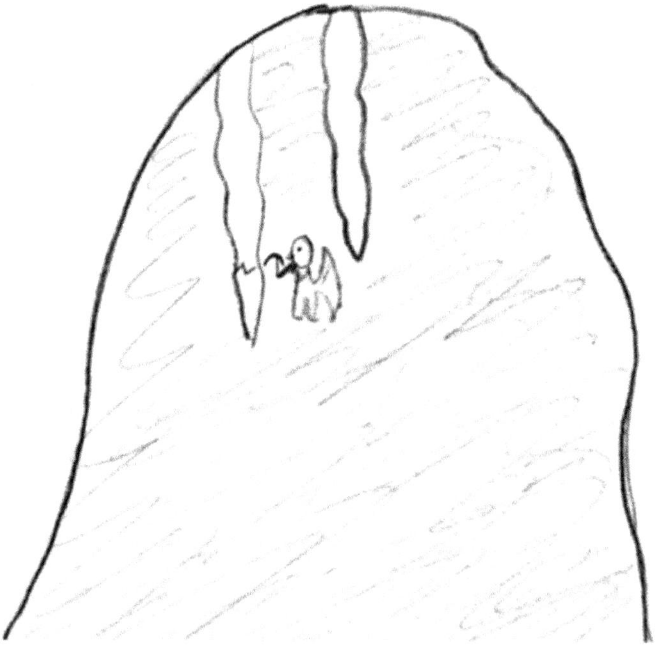

[157] REV. ELIAS OWEN, *Welsh Folk-Lore - Owen - 1887*, 86–88; MacKillop, *Dictionary of Celtic Mythology*, 83; Wirt Sikes, *British Goblins: Welsh Folk-Lore, Fairy Mythology, Legends and Traditions*, 24 & 133.

Cwn Annwn, or Dogs of the Abyss

Our next group of faeries, the *cwn annwn* or dogs of the abyss, appear in many of the tales as harbingers of death. You may also see the name translated as dogs of Hell or dogs of elf land. In some parts of Wales they are called *cwn Wwybir,* dogs of the sky, and in other places *cwn bendith y mamau* which is usually translated as faerie dogs.

In the tales, they usually appear as a pack of small red-eared white dogs, led by one larger dog. It is said that when they passed by all other dogs stop barking and run to their kennels, the birds would stop singing, and people knew that death was near.

Many times, they would howl at cross roads or at public places like taverns, and the people near who thought they were coming for them would be frozen in fear. Once the person they had come for died, they would stay in the churchyard until they were buried, and then sink into the ground to accompany them to Hell.[158]

158 Wirt Sikes, *British Goblins: Welsh Folk-Lore, Fairy Mythology, Legends and Traditions*, 233–237; REV. ELIAS OWEN, *Welsh Folk-Lore - Owen - 1887*, 92–94; MacKillop, *Dictionary of Celtic Mythology*, 108.

Cyhyraeth

Our next faerie is the *cyhyraeth,* which is also seen as *cyhiraeth* or *cyheuraeth*. She is the Welsh version of the Irish *banshee*. It is said that she will start her keening, which is a groaning instead of a wailing, to foretell a death or multiple deaths that will be caused by an epidemic or an accident. According to one person who heard it, it sounds like the groaning of a sick person who is about to die. He went on to say that, it starts in the distance, then again closer, with the third time sounding as though it was right next to him and was lowered in volume to that of a softly crying woman.[159]

In one location, she is known as the *gwrach y rhibyn*, and there she is said to haunt Pennard Castle, and the banks of the river Dribble. Other tales tell of her being heard in the ocean off the coasts, here foretelling ships sinking. One description of her reads:

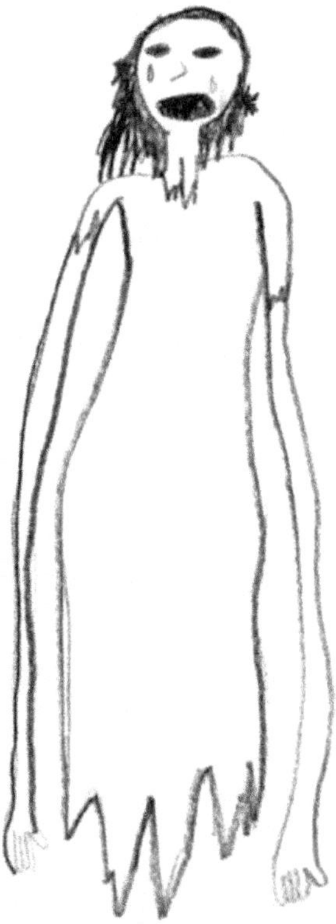

> "The picture usually given of the *Cyhiraeth* is of the most repellent kind: tangled hair, long black teeth, wretched, skinny, shrivelled arms of unwonted length out of all proportion to the body."[160]

[159] Wirt Sikes, *British Goblins: Welsh Folk-Lore, Fairy Mythology, Legends and Traditions*, 219–222.

[160] John Rhys, *Celtic Folklore - Welsh and Manx*, 252–255.

Ellyll/Ellyllon

Our next faerie is the *ellyll*, if you are referring to one fairy, or the *ellyllon*, if you are referring to more than one. This faerie looks the most like the Disney ideal of a faerie, small with wings like Tinkerbelle. They are said to live in the woods and the glens that are still wild areas. Their usual food is the toadstool, or "faerie butter," a fungus-like substance found in limestone crevices, and under the roots of rotten trees.

There is a story told about how the *ellyllon* could work magic. In it, we find Rowli Pugh, who is a poor farmer who feels himself cursed by misfortune. Other farmers flourish while his crops fail and his cattle grow thin. An *ellyll* offers to have his people help him, but only if the farmer will leave a candle burning in the night, and have his wife sweep the fire clean. The farmer complies, and the *ellyllon* make good their promise. Each night, as Rowli and his wife Catti go to bed, they hear the *ellyllon* at their merry work.

Each morning the entire household is in good order. This continues for three years. Rowli and Catti, along with their cattle and crops, become healthier and stronger. Then one night, Catti becomes curious to see the *ellyllon* at their high-spirited work. She tiptoes downstairs to the kitchen to see the faeries work. The infectious good humor of their work sets her to laughing, and she is heard by the *ellyllon*. The *ellyllon* depart quickly and never return. However, to give the story a happy ending, Rowli and Catti retain their health and prosperity with hard work.[161]

[161] Wirt Sikes, *British Goblins: Welsh Folk-Lore, Fairy Mythology, Legends and Traditions*, 13–17.

Ellylldan

Our next faerie is the *ellylldan,* which is the Welsh version of the English will-o-the-wisp. This is a common phenomenon in many parts of Wales, and it is believed that they lie in wait for unwary travelers to lead them into the bogs. As with the will-o-the-wisp, the belief may arise from the natural production and combustion of methane in boggy areas.

This faerie is described as taking the shape of a small woman with glowing lights at her finger tips, like the Bretton *sand yan y tad.* The tales describe how she would lure people into the bogs by waving her fingers at them and trying to call them to her. One writer in the late 1800's said that she was not seen much anymore due to the farmers draining all the marshes in Wales so they could use the land for farming.[162]

[162] Ibid, 18–19; Keightley, Thomas, *The Fairy Mythology*, 441.

Gwrach y Rhybin

Moving on, we come to the *gwrach y rhybin*, who is an ugly, hag-like faerie that acts like a traditional *banshee*. She is said to live in the fog, and was only seen by the person that was about to die, but the rest of the family would hear her cries. Some of the tales tell how if you hear her, but do not see her, then you will just suffer from misfortune. They also tell that when she appears before a person, she calls that person by name, so they know she has come for them.[163]

The most obvious features of all the tales about her is her ugliness. One of the stories describes her thus:

> "*Y mae mor salw a Gwrach y Rhibyn.*" (She is as ugly as the *Gwrach y Rhibyn.*) The spectre is a hideous being with dishevelled hair, long black teeth, long, lank, withered arms, leathern wings, and a cadaverous appearance."

While another describes her as:

> "...a horrible old woman with long red hair and a face like chalk, and great teeth like tusks, looking back over her shoulder at me as she went through the air with a long black gown trailing along the ground below her arms, for body I could make out none."[164]

---

163 REV. ELIAS OWEN, *Welsh Folk-Lore - Owen - 1887*, 99.

164 Wirt Sikes, *British Goblins: Welsh Folk-Lore, Fairy Mythology, Legends and Traditions*, 217–219.

Gwragedd Annwn

Next, we come to the *gwragedd annwn*, which means wives of the Otherworld, or Hell. These are similar to the English "Lady of the Lake" faeries. They are described as being beautiful maidens with long golden hair. They are said to be gentle and live harmoniously in families under the lakes, and sometimes marry mortals.

The tales are told of some of the lakes in Wales, where entire towns were once submerged, and these have now became the dwelling place of the *gwragedd annwn*. It is said that at certain times, you can see the faerie castles under the water and hear the faerie bells ringing.[165]

[165] Ibid, 33–38; Ellen Phillips, *The Enchanted World: Fairies and Elves*, 119, 122 & 127.

Gwylligi, or Dog of Darkness

Moving on, we come to the *gwylligi*, or dog of darkness. This was said to be a very large faerie dog with horrible breath and shining red eyes that burned in the dark. It was told that he was like a mastiff, but larger than a nine year old horse.

It was told that his breath was so terrible that it burned down all the grass and trees around him. Many of the stories tell about people walking along the roads at night seeing just two red eyes coming toward them, with no form under them. As they got closer, they would smell the horrible breath, and would know it was the *gwylligi*.

Those who heard the *gwylligi* in passing talked about the terror they felt when they heard the sounds and howls coming from it. In one of the tales, a man was walking with a large mastiff. When he saw the eyes, he tried to get the mastiff to protect him, but it turned tail and ran all the way home.[166]

[166] Wirt Sikes, *British Goblins: Welsh Folk-Lore, Fairy Mythology, Legends and Traditions*, 167–173; MacKillop, *Dictionary of Celtic Mythology*, 233.

Gwyllion

Our next faerie is a solitary faerie that lives in the mountains of Wales, and is known as the *gwyllion.* The *gwyllion* are frightening female faeries, who haunt lonely roads in the Welsh mountains, and lead night-wanderers astray. The Welsh word *gwyll* is variously used to signify gloom, shade, duskiness, a hag, a witch, a faerie, and a goblin, but its special application is to these mountains as places of gloomy and harmful habitats. The *gwyllion* are sometimes known as the Old Women of the Mountain.[167]

One description said that:

> "…she looked like a poor old woman, with an oblong four-cornered hat, ash-colored clothes, her apron thrown across her shoulder, with a pot or wooden can in her hand, such as poor people carry to fetch milk with, always going before the spectator, and sometimes crying 'Ww-bwb!,' which is the Welsh cry of distress. It is said that anyone who saw this apparition, whether by night or on a misty day, would be sure to lose their way, though they might be perfectly familiar with the road. Sometimes they heard her cry, 'W-bwb!' when they did not see her."[168]

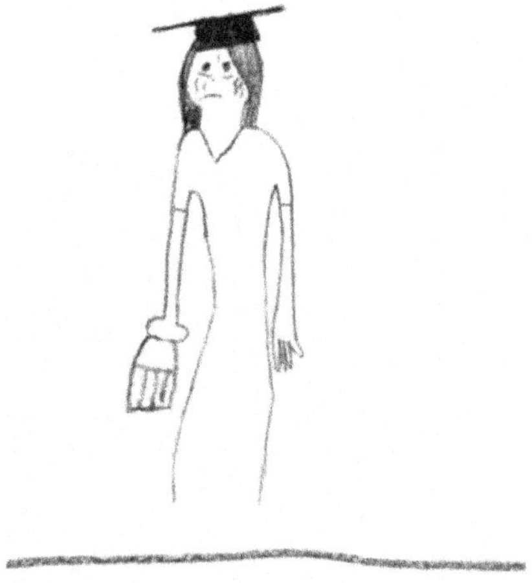

[167] Ellen Phillips, *The Enchanted World: Fairies and Elves*, 53–54.

[168] Wirt Sikes, *British Goblins: Welsh Folk-Lore, Fairy Mythology, Legends and Traditions*, 49–51.

Jili Ferwtan

Moving on we come to Jili Ferwtan. This is also seen as Jili Ffrwtan or Jili Frwtan. She is the Welsh female version of Rumpelstiltskin. There is a story told about the Jili Ferwtan coming upon a woman who didn't have time to finish her spinning. She promised to do the work, and return it to the woman, only if the woman could remember her name in three days' time when she brought the work back.

As soon as the Jili Ferwtan left, the woman forgot her name. In a panic, she set about searching for the faerie, and finally found her singing as she worked. The fairy revealed her name in the song, and the woman was able to state her name when the time came.[169]

169 MacKillop, *Dictionary of Celtic Mythology*, 247 and others.

Pwwka

Our next faerie, the *pwwka*, is another mischievous faerie that is more of a bother, that out to hurt humans. The name may also be seen as *pwca*, or *puca*. This faerie is similar to the Irish *púca* or the Cornish *bucca*. There are many tales describing the *pwwka*, but I think that for a description of how it acts, Shakespeare may have said it best in the play "A Midsummer's Night Dream," where he has Puck say:

> "I'll follow you, I'll lead you about a round,
> Through bog, through bush, through brake, through brier,
> Sometime a horse I'll be, sometime a hound,
> A hog, a headless bear, sometime a fire;
> And neigh, and bark, and grunt, and roar, and burn,
> Like horse, hound, hog, bear, fire, at every turn."[170]

There is a Welsh tradition that Shakespeare had many friends and may have visited *Cwm Pwca*, Puck's valley. Some people even think that this valley was the original inspiration for the play.[171]

[170] Wirt Sikes, *British Goblins: Welsh Folk-Lore, Fairy Mythology, Legends and Traditions*, 20–24 quoting Shakespeare.

[171] MacKillop, *Dictionary of Celtic Mythology*, 326; REV. ELIAS OWEN, *Welsh Folk-Lore - Owen - 1887*, 88–90; Wirt Sikes, *British Goblins: Welsh Folk-Lore, Fairy Mythology, Legends and Traditions*, 117–118.

Teulu

Our next faerie, the *teulu*, is really a group of faeries that are always seen together. Another name for this is the "Goblin Funeral," and this aptly describes how this is seen. A person will be out walking late and night and see a procession coming towards her. As it gets closer, she will see that it is a funeral procession. Later, it may be a few days or even weeks, she will be in the same spot during the day and see a real funeral passing by exactly as the goblin funeral did.

In several of the tales, one of the faeries will stop and talk to the person watching, and then during the real funeral, someone will really talk to the person and say the same thing. People have learned over time that seeing the goblin funeral is always an omen of impending death coming to the village.[172]

[172] Wirt Sikes, *British Goblins: Welsh Folk-Lore, Fairy Mythology, Legends and Traditions*, 231–233.

Tolaeth

For our last faerie from Wales, we have the *tolaeth*. The *tolaeth* is a ghost like creature that was only apparent to one sense at a time. When heard it could not be seen, and it could not be heard if anybody saw it in any form. As a rule, the *tolaeth* is described as rapping, or knocks, or heavy thuds. Sometimes it sounded like the shuffling or tramping of many feet, or the noise of people bearing a heavy burden.[173]

The following tale about the *tolaeth* come from South Wales.

> "A fisherman living on the shores of St. Bride's Bay said that for three successive nights in 1903 he was disturbed by the sounds downstairs of shuffling feet, doors opening, chairs being moved, and a grunting sound like that of men laying down a heavy burden or load of something. Both he and his wife agreed that they were nothing less than the *Tolaeth*. The noises were only heard in the kitchen. A week later, their only son was drowned, and his body was brought home on a ladder. The mysterious sounds were exactly reproduced…all were heard as in the solitary watches of the night." [174]

---

[173] Ibid, 225–231; REV. ELIAS OWEN, *Welsh Folk-Lore - Owen - 1887*, 301–302.

[174] Wirt Sikes, *British Goblins: Welsh Folk-Lore, Fairy Mythology, Legends and Traditions*, 226–227.

8 FAIRY CHANGELINGS

The fairy changeling is a very common theme in faerie tales and many stories have been written about it. The underlying theme in all of them is that the faeries creep into a house at night and exchange one of their babies for a human baby. There are a lot of different reasons as to why this happens, and I'll talk a little about a few of them to start this chapter.

- The faerie baby is sickly.

This appears to be one of the most used theme in the tales based on the descriptions of the babies. Many of the descriptions of the faerie baby are of a sickly baby that grows ugly. Writing in "British Goblins," Wirt Sikes tells us:

> "It grows ugly of face, shrivelled of form, ill-tempered, wailing, and generally frightful. It bites and strikes, and becomes a terror to the poor mother."[175]

It was thought that by taking a healthy human baby, the faeries would have a child that would live longer.

- The faerie baby has died.

In some of the tales, instead of a real baby, a "fetch" or "stock," which was an enchanted piece of wood, would be left in place of the child. This piece of magic would appear to grow for a while, and then appear to grow sickly and die. In this way, the human parents would not suspect their baby was a changeling. When the baby died and was buried, the fetch would turn back into a piece of wood.

- Faerie blood is weak and needs to be made stronger.

Many times, we hear that the blood of faerie had been weakening over the years and it needed an infusion of fresh, strong blood. By taking a human child and raising them as faerie, when they mated with the faeries the mixing of the genes would strengthen the faerie race.

---

[175] Ibid, 56.

- The faerie couple do not like their child.

In the chapter on Wales, we talked about the *bendith y mamau*, and their children the *crimbils*, and told how ugly they were reported to be. Since the *bendith y mamau* were known for leaving their children in exchange for human children, it is very possible that the main reason was because they didn't like their own child, and wanted a "pretty" baby.

- The human baby has a talent the faeries want.

Some of the tales talk about how the faeries could "read the future" of the human children, and know that they would have a talent the faeries enjoyed, such as music. Other tales tell us how the faeries liked to entrance talented humans to join with them for a "few days" in fairyland so they could enjoy their music or stories. Putting these stories together, it makes sense that this may have been a reason to take the baby when they were small. In this way, the faeries would strengthen the child's talent with their own teachings.

- The changeling is an old faerie that is about to die.

Some people feel that when a faerie grows old, it wishes to live a comfortable life until it dies. This is accomplished by taking the place of a human child so that it will be cuddled and cared for by human parents. This idea may come about from the old saying that when a human dies, a new faerie is born, and conversely, when a faerie dies, a human child is born.

Moving on to more information about changelings, we find that while the term changeling is the "generic" term for the child that was left, other terms have been used. For the Welsh, the child was called the *plentyn a newidiwyd*. In Ireland, the child was called the *corpán sídhe*, or *síodbhradh*, or *síofra*. In Scotland, the child was called a *tàcharan* or *ùmaidh*. And on the Isle of Man, the child was known as a *lhiannoo shee*.[176]

Since the problem of changelings was so prevalent in the past, there were many ideas about how you could prevent the exchange from happening. Some people believed that hanging an iron horseshoe, steel or iron nails, or Rowan tree branches by a baby's crib

[176] MacKillop, *Dictionary of Celtic Mythology*, 78.

would keep the faeries away. Another belief was that if you left the baby alone for too long, the faeries would come and get it. It was for this reason that when the mother left the room, she would put a set of iron fire tongs over the top of the crib to protect the child.

And yet another belief was that by putting a cross or other protective sign over the crib the faeries would stay away. It was also thought that if the mother came upon the faeries as they were taking the child, she could prevent it from happening by pulling the child into her arms, and several tales tell about this type of struggle.

If the people thought that their baby had been exchanged for a faerie baby, they had methods to prove it. Most of them were not nice at all, and were injurious to the child. One "sure" method was to hold the baby on a shovel over a fire. If he disappeared or was not burned, then he was a changeling. If his skin burned, then he was human. Another method had the baby placed in a tub of water with fox-glove plants in it. The water is said to kill a faerie child.

Still other methods included placing the child in an oven, or beating it with iron rods. In some areas, they used the same methods to find a witch, putting it in a pond and seeing if it sank. And the list of methods like this goes on to many other cruel tests.

While most of the ways to find a changeling were cruel, there were a few that were not. It was thought that if you "surprised" the baby, it would reveal itself. In the book, "British Goblins," we find the following tale:

> "A mother whose child had been stolen, and a changeling left in its place, was advised by the Virgin Mary to prepare a meal for ten farm-servants in an egg-shell, which would make the changeling speak. This she did, and the changeling asked what she was about. She told him. Whereupon he exclaimed, 'A meal for ten, dear mother, in one egg-shell?' Then he uttered the exclamation given above, ('I have seen the acorn/ etc.,) and the mother replied, 'You have seen too many things, my son, you shall have a beating/With this she fell to beating him, the child fell to bawling, and the

> fairy came and took him away, leaving the stolen child sleeping sweetly in the cradle. It awoke and said, 'Ah, mother, I have been a long time asleep!'"[177]

Another tale in the book "Legends and Romances of Brittany" shows us a similar fate:

> "Thus, on suspicion resting upon a certain Breton infant who showed every sign of changeling nature, milk was boiled on the fire in egg-shells, whereupon the impish youngster cried: 'I shall soon be a hundred years old, but I never saw so many shells boiling! I was born in Pif and Paf, in the country where cats are made, but I never saw anything like it!' Thus self-revealed, the elf was expelled from the house."[178]

Looking back to the time the idea of changelings became so widespread, it is easy to see today some of the reasons for this happening. We know that early childhood mortality was very high in those days. Most children did not even live to see their first birthday. Human nature being what it is, the people and the clergymen, did not want to think that the parents were the cause of the problem.

Rather than blame the mothers, the idea of the babies that were sickly, abnormal, or even dying soon after birth being caused by the faeries, helped the parents get through their grief. While it is suspected that this belief started among the peasants, eventually it became church teaching and the clergymen would "teach" their congregation how to protect their children.

---

[177] Wirt Sikes, *British Goblins: Welsh Folk-Lore, Fairy Mythology, Legends and Traditions*, 56 and most of chapter 5 for changeling information.

[178] Lewis Spence, *Legends and Romances of Brittany*, 83.

9 THE FAERIES HOMELANDS

There is a story told in olden days of Oisín, the son of Finn mac Cumhal. A queen from the Fairyland, Niamh Chinn Óir, Niamh of the golden Hair, looked across the seas and saw Oisín sitting by the shore. She thought that he was the most beautiful and wondrous man that she had ever seen. She knew right then that she wanted him to be her lover. She rode across the waves on her magical white horse and stopped before Oisín as he sat by the sea. She said to him:

> "You are the most wondrous man I have ever seen. Come with me to my home across the sea and be my lover. My land is the most delightful land of all that there are under the sun; the trees are stooping down with fruit and with leaves and with blossom. Honey and wine are plentiful there; no wasting will come upon you with the wasting away of time; you will never see death or lessening. You will get feasts, playing and drinking; you will get sweet music on the strings; you will get silver and gold and many jewels. You will get everything I have said … and many gifts beyond ken which I have no leave to tell."[179]

It has been said that after giving it much thought, Oisín went with her. Many interesting things happened to Oisín after that, but that's another story!

This description of the Otherworld is a powerful and vivid description of the wonders found there. The Otherworld was known by many names. It was located on islands that would appear and disappear off the shore. The Irish thought it was to the west, and called it *Tír na nÓg* (Land of the Young), *Tír na Aill* (The Other World)

---

179 Fleming and Duncan Baird Publishers, *Heroes of the Dawn*, 28.

and *Hy Brasil* (the Fortunate Island), *Tír fo-Thuinn* (Land Under the Wave), *Mag Mell* (Land of Truth), *Emain Ablach* (Isle of Apples), *Hy na-Beatha* (Isle of Life), *Tír na-m-Buadha* (Land of Virtue), *Tír na mBan* (Land of Women), *TírTairngire* (Land of Promise) and *Tír na mBéo* (Land of the Living).[180]

For the Welsh it was known as *Ynys Gwydrin* (Isle of Glass), which is also seen as *Ynys Gurtin* or *Ynys Wydrin.* Some tales place it in the Irish Channel off the Pembrokeshire coasts, while others place it on land at Glastonbury Tor. The Welsh also talked about *Ynys Afallon,* the Isle of Apples or the Happy Land, which is located in the western ocean.[181]

To the Bretons, it was the Isle of Man. And to the Scots, it was called *Lochlainn* (the Sea House or realm of dangerous invaders), or *Elphyne,* which is also seen as *Elfame.*

No matter what it was called, the descriptions are very similar. They describe the land as very beautiful, where the "Old Ones," have gone to live after leaving this plane of existence. By "Old Ones," the tales may mean the old Gods and Goddesses, people when they die, or the faeries that were not around as much.

In Ireland, *Tír na nÓg* is probably the best known of all of the Otherworlds, simply because it was used in the story of Oisín that I talked about above. That story was written down in the Middle Irish poem called "*Laoi Oisín I dTír na nÓg,*" which translates to "The Lay of *Oisín* in the Land of Youth." *Tír Na nÓg* is also mentioned in *Imram Brain*, the Voyage of Bran.[182]

Hy Brasil is also described as being in the western ocean off Ireland. It was said that this was a fog covered island that people rarely saw. According to the tales, one day every seven years the fog would blow away and even though people could see it, they still could

180 MacKillop, *Dictionary of Celtic Mythology*, 159, 237 & 358.
181 Ibid, 381.
182 Ibid, 358.

not land on it. There are reports of expeditions trying to find it, going back to the late 1400's and modern thinking places it as the Porcupine Bank which was discovered in 1862.[183]

Tír fo-Thuinn is found in the tale of *"Tóraigheacht an Ghiolla Dheacir,"* which translates as "The Pursuit of the Difficult Servant." In this story, the Fianna travel here in search of a person.

Mag Mell is described as an island paradise found to the west of Ireland. It is supposed to be the resting place of the Formorians, or in some of the tales the home of Manannán mac Lir. This island is also talked about in *Imram Brain*, the Voyage of Bran.[184]

Another island talked about in the Voyage of Bran is *Emain Ablach.* It is described as the main home of Manannán mac Lir and in some of the tales is referred to as the modern Isle of Man. This reference is not considered valid by modern scholars.[185]

Hy na-Beatha and *Tír na-m-Buadha* are referred to in a few of the older books, but not much is given on them, other than the translation of island of life, and land of virtue respectively.[186]

We find information on *Tír na mBan* in two of the *Imram* (voyage tales) — *Imram Brain*, the Voyage of Bran and *Imram Curaig Maíle Dúin*, the Voyage of Máel Dúin. In the *Imram Brain,* Bran was summoned to the island by its queen and spent some time with her. While he thought that only a single year had passed, in reality he was there for many years. In the *Imram Curaig Maíle Dúin,* Máel Dúin and his men travel to many wonderful island. On *Tír na mBan* they are served a wonderful meal, listen to fantastic music, and each find a woman to spend the night with.[187]

---

183 "Brasil (mythical Island)"; MacKillop, *Dictionary of Celtic Mythology*, 237.

184 "Mag Mell"; MacKillop, *Dictionary of Celtic Mythology*, 283.

185 "Emain Ablach"; MacKillop, *Dictionary of Celtic Mythology*, 159.

186 John O'Hanlon, *Irish Folk Lore: Traditions and Superstitions of the Country, with Humorous Tales*, 115 & 293 most other quotes refer to this book.

187 MacKillop, *Dictionary of Celtic Mythology*, 240–242 & 358; "Máel Dúin"; "The Voyage of Bran"; John O'Hanlon, *Irish Folk Lore: Traditions and Superstitions of the Country, with Humorous Tales*, 293–295.

Tír Tairngire, the Land of Promise, is probably most familiar to people today from the role-playing game Shadowrun, but it also figures prominently in many of the voyage tales. It is another of the homes of Manannán mac Lir, and was a common destination for adventures to go to find knowledge. When the *Tuatha Dé Danann* came to Ireland, they brought the rowan tree from this island with them.[188]

Tír na mBéo, the Land of the Living, is very similar to *Tír na nÓg* in its descriptions. It is another island of paradise where the *Tuatha Dé Danann* went when they left Ireland. It is said that Lúgh of the *Tuatha Dé Danann* brought his sword to Ireland from this island.[189]

In Wales, *Ynys Gwydrin,* or the Isle of Glass, is the likely the best known of the Otherworlds. For many people today, this island is synonymous with the resting place of King Arthur. While some of the tales place this in the ocean, many feel today that a more likely location was on Glastonbury Tor. Many people feel that at one time the area around the tor was flooded, so the high point would appear as an island in the plains of the land, making it a very magical place.[190]

Ynys Afallon, or as it is better known in English as Avalon, is another of the Welsh Otherworlds that has a large connection to the legend of King Arthur. Also called the Isle of Apples, this island is also connected with Glastonbury. Looking at history, this connection really came about from the writings of Cambrensis in the twelfth century. Before that, its location is given in the ocean.[191]

In Scotland, we see the Otherworld as *Lochlainn.* In the Irish tale, *Lebor Gabála Érenn,* this land is named as the home of the Formorians. Other tales place it in Scandinavia and say that the Norsemen are the inhabitants. And still other tales place it in the Gulf

---

188 MacKillop, *Dictionary of Celtic Mythology*, 358–359.
189 Ibid, 358.
190 Ibid, 381; Keightley, Thomas, *The Fairy Mythology*, 74; "Glastonbury Tor."
191 MacKillop, *Dictionary of Celtic Mythology*, 381.

of Corryvreckan, a narrow straight between two islands off the west coast of Scotland.[192]

In Scotland, we also hear about *Elphyne,* which was the name given to fairyland during the Scottish witch trials. You may also see this as *elfame*. During those trials, many of the defendants talked about knowing the Queen of *Elphyne,* and the members of her court, and of learning magic from them.[193]

All of the Otherworlds are places of magic, mystery, and many times, beings who are "not quite like us." While many times in the tales it is easy to go into the Otherworlds, most people find it hard to get out again. From Oisín's "short time," which turned out to be over three-hundred years, to the voyage tales where the stops of "only a few days," turned into years, we can see that time runs different in the Otherworlds. If you try to journey into the faerie homelands yourself, be prepared for what you might find!

---

192 Ibid, 268; "Lochlann."
193 "Fairyland."

10 CONCLUSIONS

I would like to begin this conclusion section this by talking a little about sources for further research. On the Internet today, many sites have lists of the faerie races. As with anything on the Internet, I would not trust all of them. While they may be a good place to start, and to get a list of names, not all of their information is valid.

Once you have a name to look for, I would use Google Scholar or Wikipedia, to find resources to use for further research. Many of the really good folklore books, which are listed as resources on Google Scholar or Wikipedia, were written long enough ago that their copyright has expired, and they are now available online in free PDF format.

Remember though that no one book has all the answers. To really research this topic, you need to read dozens, if not hundreds of folklore books! One good location for those free PDF editions is http://www.sacred-texts.com/neu/celt/index.htm. This is the Celtic Folklore section of the website.

And now to finish this chapter, I'd like to talk briefly about theories of what the faeries really are. There are many theories about where all the faerie legends come from, but I'm only going to cover a few of them here. New theories are coming out all the time.

The first theory deals with the idea that the faeries were real people. Many tales have come down to us about the *Tuatha Dé Danann*, or the *Tylwyth Teg*, or any of the other trooping faeries going into their faerie mounds and leaving this mortal world behind. Some think that they have worked a "glamour" over humans so that we can't get there too easily today. Others believe that they went away entirely and that only the memories remain. No matter where they went, this are one possible explanation for the faeries lack of availability today. Some scholars call this the Mythological theory.

Another theory deals with the finding of natural objects. In olden days, when a person collapsed in the fields and was not able to move part of their bodies, they were said to have been "elf-shot" or "elf-stroked" or "faerie touched." Part of this came from finding small arrowheads in the fields, believed to be elf arrows. We know today that the arrowheads found are stone points from the Neolithic era and the person in question had probably suffered from a stroke. Some scholars call this the Naturalistic theory, theory based on observation of natural phenomena.

There is yet another theory, called the Pygmy theory, which states that the faeries are the remains of an early race of humans who were very small in stature. It was thought that these people used to live in caves. This theory was prevalent in the late 1800's but has gone almost completely out of fashion today. But, after hearing about the discovery of a race of pygmy sized early humans, *Homo floresiensis,* in Indonesia on the island of Flores at the end of October, 2004, it may come back into fashion.

Another modern theory deals with the faeries coming from Atlantis. Many people believe that Atlantis explains all the "odd" legends from our past. Faeries are included in these legends. The theory goes that when Atlantis sank, the many races that lived on it spread out and that some of them became the faeries in the lands they moved to.

Finally, a theory that might very well be the most popular one today, the Alien theory. With the interest in UFO's and extraterrestrials, many people believe that visitors to this planet in the past started the legends of the faeries. And they feel that the continued visits account for the current sighting in Ireland and other countries where the faeries are strongly believed in.

And now to what I believe. I believe that the *Tuatha Dé Danann* and other races of faeries were, and still are, real people. I believe that they moved their entire tribes, including all the other beings we now know as faeries, to another reality that exists very close to our own. Finally, I know through personal experience that it is possible to get to that place where they reside, and it is possible for them to move into our reality when they want!

BIBLIOGRAPHY

"Aarne–Thompson Classification System - Wikipedia, the Free Encyclopedia." Accessed April 30, 2013. http://en.wikipedia.org/wiki/Aarne%E2%80%93Thompson_classification_system.

Alfred Perceval Graves. *The Irish Fairy Book*. London: T.F. Unwin, 1909. https://archive.org/details/irishfairybook00gravrich.

Anna Eliza Bray. *A Peep at the Pixies, or Legends of the West*. London: Grant & Griffith, 1854. http://www.sacred-texts.com/neu/eng/ppx/index.htm.

Arrowsmith, Nancy. *A Field Guide to the Little People*. New York: Hill and Wang, 1977.

Arthur William Moore. *The Folk-Lore of the Isle of Man: Being an Account of Its Myths, Legends, Superstitions, Customs, & Proverbs, Collected from Many Sources; with a General Introduction; and with Explanatory Notes to Each Chapter*. London: Brown & Sons, 1891. http://isle-of-man.com/manxnotebook/fulltext/folklore/index.htm.

Bella Terreno. "Mystical Mythology from around the World." Accessed May 8, 2013. http://www.bellaterreno.com/art/siteindex.aspx.

"Black Shuck." *Wikipedia, the Free Encyclopedia*, February 21, 2014. http://en.wikipedia.org/w/index.php?title=Black_Shuck&oldid=596560347.

"Brasil (mythical Island)." *Wikipedia, the Free Encyclopedia*, March 15, 2014. http://en.wikipedia.org/w/index.php?title=Brasil_(mythical_island)&oldid=598963446.

"Brittany Map," n.d. http://www.thetourexpert.eu/wp-content/uploads/2011/07/brittany_map_pol.gif.

Charles Hardwick. *Traditions Superstitions and Folklore of Lancaster and the North of England*. London: SIMPKIN, MARSHALL & CO., 1872. file:///c:/E-texts/Traditions__Superstitions__and_Folklore_.pdf.

Daniel Parkinson. "Black Annis | Mysterious Britain & Ireland." Accessed June 11, 2013. http://www.mysteriousbritain.co.uk/england/leicestershire/folklore/black-annis.html.

———. "Boggart | Mysterious Britain & Ireland." Accessed June 11, 2013.

http://www.mysteriousbritain.co.uk/england/folklore/boggart.html.

David Laing LL.D. *Select Remains of the Ancient Popular and Romance Poetry of Scotland*. Edited by John Small MA. Edinburgh: William Blackwood & Sons, 1885.

Donald Alexander Mackenzie. *Wonder Tales from Scottish Myth and Legend*. New York: Frederick A Stokes Co, 1917. http://www.sacred-texts.com/neu/celt/tsm/index.htm.

Douglas Hyde. *Beside The Fire: A Collection of Irish Gaelic Folk Stories*. London, 1910.

Electric Scotland. "Social History of the Highlands: Superstitions." Accessed March 5, 2014. http://www.electricscotland.com/history/social/sh3.html.

Eliza Gutch, and M. G. W. Peacock. *Examples of Printed Folk-Lore Concerning Lincolnshire*. Vol. 5. London: DAVID NUTT, 1908. http://books.google.com/books/about/Examples_of_printed_folk_lore_concerning.html?id=6kgKAAAAIAAJ.

Ellen Phillips, ed. *The Enchanted World: Fairies and Elves*. The Enchanted World. Alexandra, VA: Time-Life Books, 1984.

"Emain Ablach." *Wikipedia, the Free Encyclopedia*, August 29, 2013. http://en.wikipedia.org/w/index.php?title=Emain_Ablach&oldid=570730251.

en.wiktionary.org. "Sìthiche - Scots Gaelic." Accessed March 5, 2014. http://en.wiktionary.org/wiki/s%C3%ACthiche.

F.W. Moorman. "Yorkshire Dialect Poems." Accessed June 13, 2013. http://www.gutenberg.org/files/2888/2888-h/2888-h.htm#link2H_4_0081.

"Fairyland." *Wikipedia, the Free Encyclopedia*, March 15, 2014. http://en.wikipedia.org/w/index.php?title=Fairyland&oldid=589774144.

Fleming, Fergus, and Duncan Baird Publishers. *Heroes of the Dawn: Celtic Myth*. Amsterdam: Time-Life Books, 1996.

Franklin, Anna, Paul Mason, and Helen Field. *The Illustrated Encyclopedia of Fairies*. London: Paper Tiger, 2004.

George Fraser Black, and Northcote Whitridge Thomas, eds. *Examples of Printed Folk-Lore Concerning the Orkney & Shetland Islands, Volume 3*. London: DAVID NUTT, 1903. http://archive.org/stream/countyfolklore03folkuoft/countyfolklore03folkuoft_djvu.txt.

George Henderson. *Survivals in Belief Among the Celts*. Glascow:

JAMES MACLEHOSE AND SONS, 1911.
"Glaistig." *Wikipedia, the Free Encyclopedia*, February 15, 2014. http://en.wikipedia.org/w/index.php?title=Glaistig&oldid=570722663.
"Glastonbury Tor." *Wikipedia, the Free Encyclopedia*, March 15, 2014. http://en.wikipedia.org/w/index.php?title=Glastonbury_Tor&oldid=599326947.
Gomme, George Laurence. *The Handbook of Folklore*. London: The Folklore Society, 1890. file:///c:/E-texts/The_Handbook_of_Folklore.pdf.
"Grindylow." *Wikipedia, the Free Encyclopedia*, March 4, 2014. http://en.wikipedia.org/w/index.php?title=Grindylow&oldid=591518803.
Guerber, HA. *Myths of the Norsemen : From the Eddas and the Sagas*. New York: Dover Publications, 1992.
"Hob - Definition and More from the Free Merriam-Webster Dictionary." Accessed June 11, 2013. http://www.merriam-webster.com/dictionary/hob.
"Irish_map_ireland_counties_green.gif," n.d.
"Isle of Man Map." Accessed March 5, 2014. http://northamericanmanx.org/shared/images/isle-of-man-map.gif.
John Abercromby. "Traditions, Customs, and Superstitions of the Lewis." *Folklore* 6, #2 (June 1895): 162–71.
John Francis Campbell. *Popular Tales of the West Highlands*. London: A. Gardner, 1890. http://books.google.com/books/reader?id=SadZAAAAMAAJ&printsec=frontcover&output=reader&source=gbs_atb_hover&pg=GBS.PP1.
John Gregorson Campbell. *Superstitions of the Highlands and Islands of Scotland*. Glasgow: J. Maclehose & Sons, 1900. https://archive.org/details/superstitionshi00campgoog.
John Harland, and T. T. Wilkinson. *Lancashire Folk-Lore: Illustrative of the Superstitious Beliefs and Practices, Local Customs and Usages of the People of the County Palatine*. London: FREDERICK WARNE AND CO, 1867.
John O'Hanlon. *Irish Folk Lore: Traditions and Superstitions of the Country, with Humorous Tales*. Cameron & Ferguson, 1870.
John Rhys. *Celtic Folklore - Welsh and Manx*. Oxford: AT THE

CLARENDON PRESS, 1901. http://www.sacred-texts.com/neu/cfwm/.

Joseph Jacobs. *More English Fairy Tales*. New York; London: GP Putnam's Sons, 1911.

Joseph Wright, ed. *The English Dialect Dictionary: A-C - Google Books*. Accessed June 11, 2013. http://books.google.com/books?id=HIJBAQAAIAAJ&pg=PA605&lpg=PA605&dq=churn+milk+peg&source=bl&ots=MM0OobI6Vv&sig=prf1V1vYHHWJIuR-F0Rp764IHpM&hl=en&sa=X&ei=51m3UbCqPJbK4AON14HABg&ved=0CEMQ6AEwBA#v=onepage&q=churn%20milk%20peg&f=false.

Keightley, Thomas. *The Fairy Mythology*. London: W. H. Ainsworth, 1828.

"Kelpie." *Wikipedia, the Free Encyclopedia*, February 20, 2014. http://en.wikipedia.org/w/index.php?title=Kelpie&oldid=592869818.

Lady Francesca Speranza Wilde. *Ancient Legends, Mystic Charms, and Superstitions of Ireland*. London: Ward & Downey, 1887. http://www.sacred-texts.com/neu/celt/ali/index.htm.

Larkin, David, ed. *Faeries*. New York: Abrams, 1978.

Lewis Spence. *Legends and Romances of Brittany*. New York: FREDERICK A. STOKES COMPANY, 1917. http://www.sacred-texts.com/neu/celt/lrb/index.htm.

"Lochlann." *Wikipedia, the Free Encyclopedia*, March 14, 2014. http://en.wikipedia.org/w/index.php?title=Lochlann&oldid=595515209.

"Loireag," n.d. http://fr.wikipedia.org/wiki/Loireag.

MacKillop, James. *Dictionary of Celtic Mythology*. Oxford; New York: Oxford university press, 1998.

Mackinlay, James M. *Folklore of Scottish Lochs and Springs*. Glascow: William Hodges & Co., 1893.

"Máel Dúin." *Wikipedia, the Free Encyclopedia*, March 16, 2014. http://en.wikipedia.org/w/index.php?title=M%C3%A1el_D%C3%BAin&oldid=599929424.

"Mag Mell." *Wikipedia, the Free Encyclopedia*, March 14, 2014. http://en.wikipedia.org/w/index.php?title=Mag_Mell&oldid=570698703.

"Manx Folk-Lore and Superstitions." *Folklore* 2, #3 (September 1891): 284–313.

"Map of Scotland." Accessed March 5, 2014. http://img2.wikia.nocookie.net/__cb20120819030920/braveheart/images/a/a1/359px-Scotland_%28Location%29_Named_%28HR%29.png.

"Map of Wales." Accessed March 5, 2014. http://upload.wikimedia.org/wikipedia/commons/2/2f/Map_of_Wales.GIF.

"Map-of-England-7." Accessed March 20, 2013. http://www.globetrekkerphotos.com/gallery2/main.php?g2_itemId=5560.

Merriam-Webster Dictionary. "Faerie - Free Merriam-Webster Dictionary." Accessed December 29, 2011. http://www.merriam-webster.com/dictionary/faerie.

———. "Fairy - Free Merriam-Webster Dictionary." Accessed December 29, 2011. http://www.merriam-webster.com/dictionary/fairy?show=0&t=1325170035.

Mirino. "Viewfinder: Scottish Myths 6." *Viewfinder*. Accessed February 26, 2014. http://mirino-viewfinder.blogspot.com/2011/08/scottish-myths-6.html.

"Mourioche." *Wikipédia*, January 8, 2014. http://fr.wikipedia.org/w/index.php?title=Mourioche&oldid=69225295.

Ms. E. C. Charmichael, ed. *The Celtic Review - Volume 5 - July 1908 to April 1909*. Vol. 5. Edinburgh: Norman Macleod, 1909. https://archive.org/details/celticreview05edinuoft.

"Nicnevin or Gyre Carlin." *Wikipedia, the Free Encyclopedia*, December 13, 2013. http://en.wikipedia.org/w/index.php?title=Nicnevin&oldid=548490694.

"Oakmen." Accessed June 13, 2013. http://www.oldcorpseroad.co.uk/index.php/ghostlore-and-hauntings/31-legendary-creatures/252-oakmen.

"P. 218 Footnote - Ankou," n.d.

Paxson, Diana. "Lares and Landwights." presented at the Wiccan Fest, Ontario, Canada, June 6, 2001.

"Peg Powler." *Wikipedia, the Free Encyclopedia*, March 2, 2014. http://en.wikipedia.org/w/index.php?title=Peg_Powler&oldid=542468707.

Pillywiggins Garden. "Pilly...What? - Pillywiggins Garden." Accessed June 13, 2013.

http://www.pillywigginsgarden.com/pillywhat.html.
R. U. Sayee. "The Origins and Development of the Belief in Fairies." *Folklore* 45, #2 (June 1934): 99–143.
REV. ELIAS OWEN. *Welsh Folk-Lore - Owen - 1887*. Oswestry & Wrexham: Woodall, Minshall, & Co., 1887. http://archive.org/details/cu31924029911520.
REV. JOHN O'HANLON. *Fairy Beliefs - Irish Folklore*, 1800. http://www.oldandsold.com/articles31n/english-lore-1.shtml.
Richard Mercer Dorson. *History of British Folklore, Volume 1*. Routledge (Taylor & Francis), 1968.
Robert Hunt. *Popular Romances of the West of England: The Drolls, Traditions and Superstitions of Old Cornwall 1903 - 3rd Edition*. 3rd ed. London: Chatto and Windus, 1903.
Rose, Carol. *Giants, Monsters, and Dragons: An Encyclopedia of Folklore, Legend, and Myth*. New York: Norton, 2001.
Scotl, Uncovering. "Bean-Nighe (Washer Woman)." *Uncovering Scotland*. Accessed February 24, 2014. http://uncoveringscotland.wordpress.com/2011/08/01/bean-nighe-washer-woman/.
Sigurd Towrie. "The Trows." Accessed March 5, 2014. http://www.orkneyjar.com/folklore/trows/.
Simon Butler. "The Asrai." Accessed March 20, 2013. http://mondrem.net/myths/Asrai.html.
Sir George Douglas. *Scottish Fairy and Folk Tales*. New York: A. L. Burt Company, 1901. http://www.sacred-texts.com/neu/celt/sfft/index.htm.
T. J. Westropp. "A Study in the Legends of the Connacht Coast, Ireland." *Folklore* 28, #2 (June 30, 1917): 180–207.
———. "A Study of Folklore on the Coasts of Connacht, Ireland (Continued)." *Folklore* 32, #2 (June 30, 1921): 101–23.
"The Blue Men of the Minch." Accessed February 24, 2014. http://www.mysteriousbritain.co.uk/scotland/western-isles/folklore/the-blue-men-of-the-minch.html.
The Carmichael Watson Project, and Alexander Carmichael. "Story Entitled 'Crodh Marra' [sea-Cattle]," n.d. http://www.carmichaelwatson.lib.ed.ac.uk/cwatson/en/fulltexttranscription/3742/0/3/10/subj_cw_id:(s4095)/Crodh%20mara%20(sea-cattle)/NOTEBOOK.
THE GAELIC SOCIETY OF INVERNESS. *Transactions of the Gaelic*

Society of Inverness Vol XXVI (1904-1907). Vol. 26. Scotland: Sterling Pub., 1910. https://archive.org/details/transactions26gaeluoft.

"The Religion of the Ancient Celts: Chapter XVI. Sacrifice, Prayer, and Divination." Accessed January 2, 2011. file:///C:/E-texts/Sacred%20texts%209.0/neu/celt/rac/rac19.htm.

"The Voyage of Bran." *Wikipedia, the Free Encyclopedia*, March 14, 2014. http://en.wikipedia.org/w/index.php?title=The_Voyage_of_Bran&oldid=582263299.

Thomas Crofton Croker. *Fairy Legends and Traditions of the South of Ireland*. Edited by T. Wright. 2nd ed. London: J. Murray, 1825. http://www.sacred-texts.com/neu/celt/flat/index.htm.

Thomas Powell, ed. *Y Cymmrodor: The Magazine of the Honourable Society of Cymmrodorion*. T. Richards, 1882.

"Thrum - Definition and More from the Free Merriam-Webster Dictionary." Accessed June 13, 2013. http://www.merriam-webster.com/dictionary/thrum.

Time-Life Books. *The Enchanted World: Night Creatures*. The Enchanted World. [Alexandria, VA : Morristown, N.J: Time-Life Books] ; School and library distribution by Silver Burdett Co, 1985.

———. *The Enchanter World: Water Spirits*. Edited by Ellen Phillips. The Enchanted World. Alexandria, VA: Time-Life Books, 1985.

W.A. Craigie. "Donald Bán and the Bócan." *Folklore* 6, #4 Dec. of 1895 (1895): 353–58.

Walter Gregor. *Folk-Lore of the North-East of Scotland*. London: ELLIOT STOCK, 1881. http://www.sacred-texts.com/neu/celt/nes/index.htm.

Walter Scott. *Minstrelsy of the Scottish Border, Vol. I (of 3): Consisting Of Historical And Romantic Ballads, Collected In The Southern Counties Of Scotland; With A Few Of Modern Date, Founded Upon Local Tradition*, 1806. http://www.gutenberg.org/cache/epub/12742/pg12742.txt.

———. *Minstrelsy of the Scottish Border, Vol. II (of 3): Consisting Of Historical And Romantic Ballads, Collected In The Southern Counties Of Scotland; With A Few Of Modern Date, Founded*

Upon Local Tradition, 1806. http://www.gutenberg.org/cache/epub/12882/pg12882.txt.

———. *The Lady Of The Lake*. Boston: J.C. Byers, 1883. http://www.gutenberg.org/cache/epub/3011/pg3011.txt.

WB Yeats. *Fairy and Folk Tales of the Irish Peasantry*. New York: T H E W A L T E R S C O T T P U B L I S H I N G C O . , L T D ., 1888. http://www.sacred-texts.com/neu/yeats/fip/index.htm.

———. , ed. *Irish Fairy Tales - Yeats 1892*. London: T. Fisher Unwin, 1892.

"wikipedia.org/wiki/Pillywiggin - French Edition." Accessed June 13, 2013. http://translate.google.com/translate?hl=en&sl=fr&u=http://fr.wikipedia.org/wiki/Pillywiggin&prev=/search%3Fq%3DPillywiggin%26client%3Dfirefox-a%26hs%3Dy9p%26rls%3Dorg.mozilla:en-US:official%26channel%3Dfflb.

William Alfred Dutt. *Highways and Byways in East Anglia*. London: Macmillan, 1901. https://ia600308.us.archive.org/24/items/highwaysbywaysin00duttuoft/highwaysbywaysin00duttuoft.pdf.

William Bottrell. *Traditions and Hearthside Stories of West Cornwall, Vol. 2*. BEARE AND SON, 1873. http://www.sacred-texts.com/neu/celt/swc2/index.htm.

WILLIAM CASHEN. *MANX FOLK-LORE*. G. & L. JOHNSON, PRINTERS & PUBLISHERS, 1912.

William Elliot Griffis. *Welsh Fairy Tales - Griffis - 1921*. New York: Thomas Y Crowell, 1921. http://archive.org/details/griwels.

Wirt Sikes. *British Goblins: Welsh Folk-Lore, Fairy Mythology, Legends and Traditions*. London: SAMPSON LOW, MARSTON, SEARLE, & RIVINGTON, CROWN, 1880. http://www.gutenberg.org/ebooks/34704.

WY Evans-Wentz. *The Fairy-Faith in Celtic Countries*. Gerrards Cross: Colin Smythe, 1911. http://books.google.com/books/about/The_fairy_faith_in_Celtic_countries.html?id=Jyoaa2ZN0qYC.

INDEX

H

J

K

P

Q

R

S

ABOUT THE AUTHOR

Robert Lee (Skip) Ellison has been interested in all things Celtic since early childhood. Since he retired, he has traveled, led an International Druid Church, given classes on many subjects, and written four books, with this as his fifth. One of his favorite classes to give is called "Dragon's, and Faeries, and Giant's, Oh My!" The idea for this book comes from that class, and more books are planned from it. In his spare time, he maintains the land and gardens on his seventeen acre property called "Dragon's Keep Farm."

The illustrator, Rhiannon Ellison, is Skip's thirteen year old granddaughter and helps with his projects. She has had a love of drawing for many years.

www.ingramcontent.com/pod-product-compliance
Lightning Source LLC
Chambersburg PA
CBHW060506290526
45791CB00001B/296
* 9 7 8 1 4 9 7 4 3 0 2 3 5 *